Startups For Outsiders
Your guide to building a scalable business
Amardeep Parmar

Bae HQ

First published in Great Britain in 2025

© Copyright Amardeep Parmar

All rights reserved. No part of this publication may be reproduced, stored in or introduced into a retrieval system, or transmitted in any form, or by any means (electronic, mechanical, photocopying, recording or otherwise) without the prior written permission of the publisher.

The right of Amardeep Parmar to be identified as the author of this work has been asserted by him in accordance with the Copyright, Designs and Patents Act 1988.

This book is sold subject to the condition that it shall not, by way of trade or otherwise, be lent, resold, hired out, or otherwise circulated without the publisher's prior consent in any form of binding or cover other than that in which it is published and without a similar condition including this condition being imposed on the subsequent purchaser.

Disclaimer

The content of this book is for information only. It does not and is not intended to constitute financial advice. You should undertake your own research and analysis, and take independent financial advice from a professional before making any decisions or investments, based on your personal circumstances. Neither Bae HQ nor the author can be held liable in respect of any damage, expense, other loss or adverse effects you may suffer as a consequence of relying on the information provided in this book.

Contents

Introduction   VII
    Who is "Startups for Outsiders" for?
    Why I'm relevant for you
    What to expect
    Starting a startup
    The best way to learn

1. Preparing to execute   1
    Sculpting a founder mindset
    Going all-in
    Deciding to have a cofounder
    What to look for in a cofounder
    Where to find cofounders
    How to test the relationship
    How to maintain the relationship
    Summary

2. Obsessing over problems and customers   26
    Discovering problems
    Shortlisting problems
    Researching customers
    Decision time
    The transformation
    Early vs ideal customers

      Research never ends
      Summary

3. Iterating to a solution   45
      Build. Build. Build.
      Launch. Launch. Launch.
      Test. Test. Test.
      Iterate. Iterate. Iterate.
      Summary

4. Earning attention   54
      Brands aren't forever
      Be the only choice
      Hero's journey
      Word of mouth
      Doing things that don't scale
      Do things that scale
      Clean up
      Press
      Summary

5. Managing finances   70
      Bootstrapping
      Maximising revenue over profit
      Customers > users
      Metrics that matter
      Business models
      Breakdown of costs
      Opening the floodgates
      Summary

6. Staying on and going off track   86
      Setting a long-term vision

>
> Short-term targets
> Preventing overwhelm
> Iterating and pivoting
> Signals to pivot
> 7 ways to pivot
> Pulling off a pivot
> Summary

7. Planning on one page — 99
   - One Page Startup script
   - Summary

8. Networking — 107
   - Resourceful
   - Specific
   - Visible
   - Powerful
   - Summary

9. Hiring early employees — 117
   - You are the example
   - Who to hire
   - Where to find them
   - What to look for
   - Retaining the best people
   - Summary

10. Funding from external sources — 129
    - Types of funding
    - Payback-free
    - Debt
    - Equity
    - Summary

11. Pitching investors — 147
    4 C's Checklist
    The Traction-Team Tilt
    How the process works
    Valuations
    Pitch deck slides
    Founder-
    Summary

12. Winning when you exit — 162
    Types of
    IPOs
    Exit
    Summary

Conclusion and Thanks — 174
  Acknowledgments
  Thank you

Introduction

Humble startups founded by people like you have changed the world. They all started somewhere, no matter how impressive they seem today. Do you believe you can build the next big thing? Humanity needs more people like you.

So many startup outsiders dream of ways to solve significant problems, but never bring them into reality. You can choose to look for reasons why you shouldn't bother. Every entrepreneur you aspire to has doubted themselves at some point. Maybe you didn't go to a fancy school. Maybe you don't know anyone. Maybe you don't think you look the part. Most startups fail anyway.

The brave among you will start despite your doubts. Yet you're entering the game without knowing the rules. No one prepared you. Everything you do is less effective. You're frustrated. You look for advice, but the startup world is full of noise. You try to make sense of the never-ending stream of dodgy guru wisdom and semi-true success stories. How are you supposed to tell apart the lightning insights from the outright filthy lies? Your odds of success erupt when you know enough to make informed decisions. That's why I've written this. I want you to win.

My goal is to make this the most useful book you read at the start of your journey. I'll guide you from outsider to insider in the most effective way I can. I've spoken to thousands of early-stage founders, and I know where the crucial knowledge gaps lie. To set expectations, you won't instantly become a billion-dollar founder on the last page. I'd charge you a lot more if it did! I can't work hard for you, nor can I control your luck, but I can help you work smarter.

Who is "Startups for Outsiders" for?

No product will please everybody, and this book is no different. You can still enjoy the insights and apply where relevant if you're not my ideal reader, but I've written this for who it says on the front cover.

First, this book is for people who are interested in building high-growth startups in the tech industry, which aim to be worth at least tens of millions (and far beyond) in only a few years. This includes deeptech and biotech, which are based on advanced scientific breakthroughs. They can be research-heavy for a long time, but have the potential for a spectacular payoff.

Second, this book is for outsiders. First-time startup founders begin as outsiders before graduating to insiders with experience over time (and revenue and capital!). The exception is when you've been an early employee elsewhere with responsibility. Some graduate from outsider to insider in no time because of privileged access to a network or money. Life's not fair. But most aren't so lucky, and this book is for you. You're welcome here for whatever reason you feel like an outsider. Insiders can skim to refresh and find fresh insights, and then gift it to a friend earlier in their journey! I hope you'll wish you had this book when you started.

I'll give you one of my favourite examples of an outsider turned insider. Dimple Patel sits on our board. She's a South Asian woman who was raised in a rough area in northern England. Statistically, these traits aren't famous for being backed in the startup space. Yet she has sold two companies and become CEO of another, which is worth over $100m. She defied the odds, and I hope you will too!

Why I'm relevant for you

Too many business books spend more time massaging the author's ego than providing valuable insights for the reader. My worst nightmare is you feeling I'm the same when you reach the last page. Your time is precious, and you need to trust that I know what I'm talking about to make this worth reading. So I'm getting all my icky humblebragging out of the way now.

My journey is a total fluke. I grew up in a diverse melting pot in East London and was far from what anyone would consider cool at school. Most of the time, I was trying my best to hide my insecurity and social anxiety. I didn't do a great job, but I belonged and could stay out of trouble. Studying Economics at the University of Bath was a harsh shift from what I knew. The posher backgrounds of many of my classmates made me feel out of place through no fault of their own. I learned to adapt, but even today, my accent jumps around subconsciously depending on who I'm with.

I thought getting a graduate job offer would be easy. I was on course for a First-Class degree with honours from a top university and had spent a year working at the Bank of England during a gap in my degree. I was wrong. I smashed the assessments, landed 50+ interviews, but always failed at the final stage. I seemed incapable of proving I'd be a cultural fit. All my university friends were getting jobs as I flailed around. Not great for my insecurity.

I finally landed a job in technology consulting, where I stayed for almost 7 years. I worked for a small firm that had giant enterprise clients. I learned so much there, but I knew I didn't want to stay forever. The problem was that I didn't know what direction to go.

I followed the good boy route: good high school grades, a good degree at university and a good consulting job in the city. I was unfulfilled but too scared to take a leap into an unorthodox career. I spent my whole life trying to fit in. Entrepreneurship wasn't for people like me - or so I believed.

My break came after a New Year's Resolution in 2020, close to my 28th birthday. My plan was to start writing online as a challenge to improve how I structured my thoughts. I didn't expect it to go anywhere, but my first article went viral. Millions read my articles over the next two years. Only Barack Obama gained followers faster than I did among writers who started in the same period on the world's largest blogging platform. I became editor of a key publication for founders, which opened my eyes to a new world. I quit my job as my online income outpaced my day job with the support of my loved ones. I experimented a lot in the first year of self-employment. I launched two podcasts where I interviewed the likes of the founders of Netflix and Twitter, and ghostwrote for over 100 startups.

Then everything changed. My dad died in the summer of 2022. He was my biggest supporter and taught me so much. I craved deeper meaning and to honour his legacy. I cofounded Bae HQ as the community for high-growth Asian-Heritage founders and investors two months later. We're the undisputed leader in our niche and one of the most prolific startup communities in the UK within three years of launching.

- 7,000+ people have attended our events and talks.

- 200+ people have been through our impact programmes, including mentorships, incubators, and school initiatives.

- 250+ episodes have been released of our podcast Startups Inside Out.

- We've worked with everyone from megafunds to big tech, banks to top universities, and international news to the government.

I've personally invested in startups as an angel investor and in venture capital funds as a small limited partner. You can find more about me and my current portfolio at www.amardeepparmar.com. My value lies in the breadth of my experience in a short period, which means I still understand what it's like at the beginning. I know what it feels like to be an outsider, and I don't want you to feel the same. I've made a lot of mistakes and squeezed insights out of hundreds of founders, operators and investors, so you don't have to. Don't expect me to have all the answers! It's smart for you to use multiple sources of information you trust to guide you.

What to expect

Entrepreneurship is chaos and doesn't follow a straight path. I've ordered the chapters to form a desirable route for most, but feel free to jump around to the parts most relevant to you now. Do what you want - I'm not your boss!

- **Chapter 1** - Understanding what it takes on a personal level to succeed at the startup game and picking your cofounders.

- **Chapter 2** - Finding a problem worth solving and how to assess what a strong idea looks like.

- **Chapter 3** - Iterating through solutions until you're able to find product-market fit.

- **Chapter 4** - Earning attention and gaining your early customers through a variety of distribution channels.

- **Chapter 5** - Managing your finances and picking the best business model for your needs.

- **Chapter 6** - Setting long-term and short-term goals and reading the signals for when it's time to pivot and how to do it.

- **Chapter 7** - Bringing together everything you've done so far into a one-page business plan, which brings to an end the first act.

- **Chapter 8** - How to build an effective network and get prioritised by busy people who you believe can help you scale.

- **Chapter 9** - Hiring your early employees, including what to look for and mistakes you should avoid.

- **Chapter 10** - Examining different external sources of funding and where they align with your ambitions.

- **Chapter 11** - How to convince investors to bet on your business, including fundamentals and pitch deck creation.

- **Chapter 12** - Preparing for a potential exit and understanding what your options in the market are.

There are exercises at the end of each chapter, and you can find further resources at www.startupsforoutsiders.com. The only task for you during this introduction is to set aside the 2-3 hours it takes to read this and commit! Send me a selfie with a 100-word review when you're done to amar@thebaehq.com and I'll add the best to the site. P.S. I've structured this to be different to other books you're recommended, I've avoided:

- Overloading you with detailed case studies (which become filler).

- Influencing you with research papers (which give false certainty).

- Spamming you with adverts for expensive programmes.

Starting a startup

Here's some comfort for you - starting isn't the hardest part of this journey. You can begin anonymously at low risk if you choose to. You can do most of the first half of this book while dabbling on the side of your job or studies. You don't have to go all-in until you're ready.

Yet to get anywhere, you have to make the decision to start. I'm not one of those annoying people on social media who will tell you startup life is for everyone regardless of their circumstances. I don't believe it is. "Startup" for the context of this book refers to the high-growth use of the term in the tech world primarily. It sounds sexier than other types of businesses, and you'll come across many people claiming to build one who aren't. I'm not. Scaling to millions and millions of revenue fast sounds impressive, but it's a load of stress and uncertainty. It doesn't make you any less if you don't want to take on that burden. I'd be insincere if I presented startups as the only choice for you if you're looking to take on a new challenge. We aren't going to cover any of the other options in detail, but you can explore for a comparison point:

- **Hobby** - A project just for fun with no intention to make significant money.

- **Charity** - A project with the primary purpose of impact, though you can pay yourself.

- **Side-hustle** - A way to make a little bit of money on the side with the optional intention of becoming a lifestyle business one day.

- **Lifestyle business** - A significant source of income where the founder is optimising for their passions and lifestyle more than profits.

- **Traditional business** - A major source of income with a profit-maximising focus.

A good chunk of you will never build any of these in a serious way. You could just love learning about this world, and you do you. I'm sure True Crime fans don't actually want to commit murder, even if they love the content about it.

Motivations to start a startup

People get into startups for all different reasons, but some are better than others. It's not worth the effort for the wrong reasons, and let's get these out of the way first:

- **To be cool** - You'll impress fewer people than you expect by becoming a founder. If they flock to you once you're successful, then you've hardly gained meaningful friends.

- **To get rich quick** - Founders often underpay themselves for years, then don't get the big exit they hoped for. There are way easier ways to get rich.

- **To be free** - You're technically your own boss, but in reality, you answer to your cofounders, investors, customers, stakeholders, and many more unless you want to be broke.

- **To avoid burnout** - Have you ever met a startup founder?!

- **To prove someone wrong** - You could join the club of founders driven by toxic reasons, but (spoiler) your "success" can feel empty at the end.

- **To please someone else** - It's your life. Don't make important life decisions because of what your friends/partner/family want you to do.

You wouldn't be alone if you start for one reason and your motivation changes over time. The best reasons to start a startup:

- **Obsession with the problem** - You can't stop thinking about the problem and the people affected. You feel irrationally driven to find a solution.

- **Joy of building** - You love the act of innovating and taking on tasks which scare others away. It makes you feel alive to deal with the uncertainty.

Other reasons which work only if you're financially secure enough to take the risk and not be bothered if it doesn't work out:

- **Building generational wealth** - You can get rich by working for others, but it's difficult to create the kind of wealth that allows you to choose never to work again unless you're an owner.

- **A new challenge** - You're bored and you've never built a startup before, so you want to experiment.

The best way to learn

If you decide to go all-in and build your dream startup, you'll realise there's no replacement for first-hand experience. I wish you all the best, and you can always refer back to this book whenever you need it. You definitely don't need to memorise it cover-to-cover to get going.

A recurring theme which comes up in several chapters is using the right tactics at the right time. The early phases of startup life, when it's just you in a coffee shop, are incomparable to running a hundred-person organisation. You can be messy and experimental at the start, then build systems and processes later. I'm more focused on the building from a coffee shop entrepreneur than the scaleup entrepreneur in these pages. You're entering a world of reinvention. What gets you to one stage won't get you to the next.

The long-term success of this book will be based on some of you changing the world and telling others that Startups for Outsiders helped you get started. I'm excited to find out what you get up to. Remember, you aren't alone. There are many communities across the world to help outsiders like you when you're ready. Now let's get started.

Chapter 1
Preparing to execute

I'm going to attack a commonly held belief by outsiders about startups straight away. Let's use an oversimplified formula:

Idea x Execution x Luck = Results

The trouble with this equation is that it implies each part has equal weighting. Outsiders overvalue ideas. Anyone can come up with ideas, but few will execute them effectively. Fewer will have luck on their side. Execution is the most important part of the equation within your control. A superstar founding team will keep adapting ideas until they strike gold. That's who you want to be!

The fatal mistake I see outsiders make is obsessing over coming up with an idea rather than sharpening their tools. Training your founder mindset means you're more capable of solving a high-potential problem at scale.

A second mistake is not putting enough weight on who you're going to build with. Most billion-dollar companies had more than one cofounder. Your ability to find the right people to start with is critical. You can go solo and hire people to fill your gaps, but you should be informed before choosing that path.

Think about it like playing a sport. The strongest team with the best execution wins the majority of the time. You can have the best strategy in the world, but you'll lose if your team is incapable of following through. Likewise, teams with unremarkable tactics can win if their players are world-class. There are freak situations where luck becomes the overwhelming factor, but you can't rely on that. This chapter is about getting you into the founder mindset, and then engaging others to join you.

Sculpting a founder mindset

Successful founders aren't clones of each other, but you'd struggle to find a cofounding team where none of them had these traits. They may not have started with them - I definitely didn't. You'll face a steep learning curve as a first-time founder, and the sooner you get your head in the game, the better. I won't cover any hard skills here, like coding languages, because they keep changing. With a growth mentality, you can adapt your thinking to any of the following:

Bias toward action

The doers change the world while the dreamers are lost in their thoughts. Customers, investors and partners will demand action. Staying still means falling behind in a competitive environment. You don't realise how much is handled for you when you work for someone else. Part of the stress of being a founder is pushing the business forward while managing endless tiny decisions. You have to get used to acting fast without overthinking the small stuff.

Training: Every time you find yourself putting off making a decision, in under a minute, decide if it's reversible or irreversible. Most decisions won't matter in 5 years, and you can change directions if they cause any trouble. At random, select a default choice, and if within a set time limit, you don't make a choice, you go with the default. Jeff Bezos popularised this framework at Amazon.

Unorthodoxy

Startup founders are rarely normal. You're attempting to bring a new innovation into the world. Everything obvious has already been done. You've got to spot a gap others haven't and be delusional enough to think you can succeed where others can't. You might have spent most of your life trying to fit in, but as a founder, you've got to stand out. Embrace what makes you unique because no one can compete with you at being you.

Training: Be different. Stop trying to fit in and lean into all your random interests and curiosities. The magic happens when you can combine lessons from one seemingly unrelated topic with another. Draw inspiration from sources others would never expect. Dream up ways to improve anything which annoys you.

Resourcefulness

When I was a developer, there was an abbreviation I loved. RTFM. Read The Fucking Manual. Becoming an entrepreneur is a choice, not an entitlement. Fall in love with solving problems because you can't expect everyone else to fix them for you. You can find the answers to almost anything with modern search engines and AI. Inhale content from those you trust. You're doing that right now by reading this book. Be the person others believe will find a way, no matter what.

Training: Teach yourself a new skill. Use free online tutorials and get as creative as you can. The reality of being a developer in the past was being exceptional at searching online for issues and figuring out how to apply the advice to your situation. How far can you get before asking for help?

Resilience

Failure is part of every founder's life. There will be many rejections, curveballs and crises along the way. You need to get used to it. I can't protect you - no one can. The ones who win keep picking themselves up. Your past experiences can prepare you - what's the hardest thing you've ever done? Bounced back from a serious illness? Survived a war? Overcome trauma? They prove you've got fire in your belly to keep going.

One great example of resilience is Radha Vyas. Her startup Flash Pack went into administration because of global travel bans just after having her first child. She went from £20m in revenue to zero. But they turned it around and smashed their pre-crisis revenue!

Training: Games are a cheat code to building resilience without putting yourself in any real danger. You could choose sports, online gaming or whatever you like. If you want to make it a solo pursuit, you could set yourself a challenge like running a marathon or climbing a mountain. Whatever it is must be beyond what you're capable of today. You're going to suck at the start, and you'll lose more than you win. Keep going anyway. Prove to yourself that you can keep failing and eventually succeed.

Magnetism

No matter how fancy the technology, you won't get far if no one wants to have a relationship with you. The founders who communicate with empathy seem to glide where others sweat. Relationships are at the centre of it all:

- **Cofounders** - Don't want to work with assholes.

- **Customers** - Don't want to buy from assholes.

- **Employees** - Don't want to work for assholes.

- **Investors** - Don't want to give money to assholes.

- **Partners** - Don't want to commit to assholes.

Training: Charisma can be learned - trust this former socially awkward dweeb. I started podcasting because I was insecure about the way I spoke, and I used to freak out in busy crowds. Put yourself in social situations and try to read people's emotions. First, appreciate others, see the world through their lens. When do they lean in? When do they flinch? You can learn so much by observing and empathising. Frame your perspective in a way they can relate to, and they'll be willing to spend much more time with you!

Focus

Too many founders are concerned with busyness rather than building a business. Run experiments to figure out what works, then focus on doing that over and over. Your to-do list will be full of high-value tasks one day. Every extra errand or event you agree to means something else important won't get done. Focus is about relentless prioritisation and only working on what's most important. It means rejecting good opportunities to take on extraordinary ones. Founders who get lost in shiny objects lose to those who stay on track.

Training: Get into the habit of prioritising different tasks across your life. There are frameworks galore on this, so find one you like. The key is determining if an ask isn't important and saying "no" quickly. Check out Chapter 6, too.

Self-Awareness

The one skill which binds all the others together. There are two parts:

1. **Your competency** - You never want to be the last person to realise when you're underperforming. Knowing where your weaknesses are

means you can either improve or delegate to the rest of the team. Understanding your strengths is as important. You have to lean into these to stand out.

2. **Your wellbeing** - You can't play at the top of your game for long if you're not physically, emotionally and mentally healthy. If you ignore the early warning signs, they will come back to haunt you.

Training: Track your performance in different tasks. Ask for feedback from those around you who are unafraid to tell it how it is. You'll have to dive deeper, if there's a big divide between how you think you're doing vs how others perceive you. P.S. You may get your feelings hurt.

Going all-in

No outsider casually builds a billion-dollar company while working 9-5 in the corporate world. You can dabble to begin with, but one day you'll need to become a full-time founder. Getting clear on what conditions need to be true for you to take the leap is crucial. This is the first test of your self-awareness because your circumstances are unique and only you know them. There's no golden rule to follow. I've outlined some questions to help you think it through.

Remember this moment is one of millions in your long life. Your answers will change over time. The perfect time to take the leap could be now, or it could be in 10 years. While we love to define ourselves by what we do, remember that identity and what matters most to you are fluid. Quitting my job terrified me. I had sleepless nights and anxiety for months. Yet the decision transformed my life and opened up experiences in a way I wouldn't have dared imagine. I never thought I'd write a book, and yet here we are.

What are your backup plans?

Beware of survivorship bias. You'll hear from founders who burnt all alternatives, so they had to make their business work, and it did. You won't hear from the majority who did this and failed. My former bosses told me that I could come back if I wanted to, if self-employment didn't work for me. I'm forever grateful for the offer, as it gave me the freedom to fail with a safety net.

Can you afford this now?

Take an honest look at your expenses and your commitments. You're unlikely to have a dependable income at the start, and it could take years before you're paying yourself your market value. What's your personal runway? How long could you go without paying yourself?

There are nuances to this, and you could build while taking a part-time role on the side. I had years of personal savings through investments and side hustle earnings. I'd be the biggest hypocrite to tell you to take a risk I didn't take. Some founders have wealthy parents who will support them, so they don't need to worry about financial concerns. Be careful of comparing the hazards you take with others who might not be risking as much.

Who else does your decision affect?

We don't live in a vacuum. You may have children, elderly parents or others who depend on you. Pretending we all have the same trade-offs isn't true. No one can tell you what you should prioritise. Plenty of founders with young children build transformational startups, so you shouldn't let it stop you. You need to be honest with yourself about how you'll compete with founders who are commitment-free. Plan for how to manage your other priorities, whatever they are.

Would more experience help you?

This advice won't be popular, but it does reflect reality. Depending on your industry, experience has a massive impact on your ability to disrupt the status quo. No one is going to invest in a biotech where none of the founders have any credibility in the sector. Fintech founders with no experience at a financial institution are going to have a rough time convincing anyone their money is safe with them. You can build domain expertise (and get paid) working for another company in the space. You can start to build a network to help guide you. You can work for another early-stage company to understand how startup life works.

Enthusiastic and intelligent young people can create generational companies. Yet many founders who achieve success start later in their careers. The popular college dropout stories of Bill Gates and Mark Zuckerberg are the exception, not the norm.

Do you need to prioritise your health?

Startups can be long hours and high stress, and can take a toll on the best of us. There's no shame in deciding you need stability right now for your well-being, whether mental or physical. Nutrition, sleep, hormone balance and stress levels are just some of the factors which impact your effectiveness as a founder. My health dipped significantly during the first two years of Bae HQ. I've managed to pull it back now, but it took me longer than I'd like to admit. Learn from my mistakes, look after your health! Seek professional advice where needed.

This doesn't mean you shouldn't build a startup if you have a long-term health condition. Just plan for how you will manage it. There is a growing number of specialist programmes which support entrepreneurs with mental or physical conditions too.

Are you willing to sacrifice fun?

Startup life isn't for everyone. You might quit the 9-to-5 for a 24/7. Do you really want to throw all your time into something which is likely not to work out? You'll have to make so many sacrifices. It's taken me several years to take time off without feeling guilty.

Deciding to have a cofounder

You've now got a sense of the founder mindset and the timing for you to go all-in. But there are more pieces to the execution puzzle. Building your startup with the right cofounders can be the difference between unbelievable success and complete and utter failure.

When I refer to cofounders, I mean co-owners in the startup from the early days. Some leaders join years later and request the cofounder title as part of their package. Yet the earlier a cofounder gets involved, the more ownership they'll feel of the company. Your optimal window is anywhere up to raising funding or making meaningful revenue. It's harder for you to see a cofounder who joins after this as a deserved equal.

I've been with my cofounder for 3 years now, and neither of us would have built Bae HQ without the other. You can build a billion-dollar company by yourself in theory, but you'd be playing in ultra-hard mode. You'd need to wear all the hats to a world-class level, as it's tough enough with cofounders! Let's map out all the different pros and cons:

Competency coverage

Your cofounder team needs someone to build the tech, someone to get customers to care and someone to make sure it makes money. These could all be one person, but it's a lot of different hats. Cofounders who shine in a variety of areas improve the overall capability of the startup.

A common debate is about whether non-technical founders can succeed alone. There are significant disadvantages. Technical cofounders mean far shorter feedback loop cycles and they can assess the quality of technical hires or agencies. Yet exceptional solo founders can teach themselves any skill they need. For example, Sandrine Zhang Ferron learnt how to code herself to build her online marketplace Vinterior; it now makes millions in revenue. Later on, you can hire specialists to take over once you have revenue or funding.

Shared load

Outsiders aren't told how many random tasks there are to handle when running a startup. All the unglamorous tasks stack up and ideally need a founder to take ownership - e.g. taxes, legals, safeguarding. Splitting these up can take a significant burden off your shoulders. You'll be surprised by how many events there are once you start building a network too. My cofounder and I can divide and make appearances across town on the same evening.

Wider perspective

All founders take insights from their personal life experiences, but this can lead to biases. I'm guilty of thinking I have a representative point of view when my circumstances don't reflect my target customers at all. Extra cofounders mean a wider range of insights and fewer blind spots.

Emotional support

Too many "entrepreneur" personalities gloss over how brutally stressful the early days of startup building are. You get rejected constantly. You doubt yourself. You wonder if you should give up. Having someone with you on the same journey who understands what you're going through can stop you from quitting.

Accountability

If you've ever had a boss, you're aware that not everyone is as approachable as they think they are. You can accidentally surround yourself with people who are afraid to call you out when you're making a mistake. Cofounders have a special place in the business where this power dynamic shouldn't exist. They own significant equity and have a voice to keep you in check.

Conflict

Cofounders can be your best friends but also your worst enemies. I won't pretend I haven't seen relationships turn ugly and bitter. Like a marriage, you can be 100% sure you're tying the knot with the right person and be proven 100% wrong in no time.

Reputation risk

Who you pick as cofounders is a reflection on you. If you pick entrepreneurs with questionable ethics, then people will either think you share the same views or that you were too naive to see. Neither is a look you want. This poor choice can linger with you longer than you might like.

Indecision

Cofounders get in each other's way when they can't make decisions independently. My cofounder and I have traded the CEO role. Whoever is the CEO is empowered in 90% of situations, with only irreversible doors needing dual approval. This system works for us, but many cofounders fail to figure out a process for themselves.

Equity split

Having cofounders means giving up a % of the pie. Let's assume equal equity amongst cofounders:

- One founder = 100% each

- Two founders = 50% each

- Three founders = 33% each

- Four founders = 25% each

Although you own less of the startup in relative terms, the hope is that the value of your slice is greater overall. Put simply, it's better to own 25% of a £100m company than 100% of a £1m company. Be aware that if you take multiple funding rounds, the total pot for founder equity can be considerably smaller. Judging whether an additional cofounder will make the valuation potential rise enough to offset what they're taking is impossible to do with any certainty. Your gut being wrong can have enormous consequences.

Cash flow needs

More people, more expenses. This is true even before founders start to take meaningful salaries. It stacks up whether it's because you need more subscriptions or to pay for extra tickets to conferences. Cofounders, in theory, can put off salaries until cash flow allows, but this can't happen forever. You need greater cash flow to pay the wages for multiple founders compared to a solo founder.

What to look for in a cofounder

Before you go out there trying to find a cofounder, you first need to have the criteria of what to look for.

Founder mindset

You'll need to assess any potential cofounders in the same way you've analysed yourself. Look to cover your weaknesses. The more challenging part is separating those who think they have what it takes from those who actually do. It's a long journey, and you don't want someone who will give up once the honeymoon phase is over. If you were an investor, would you invest in this cofounder?

Questions to ask:

- What's the hardest thing you've ever done?
- What's your greatest failure? How did you recover?
- What character traits make you believe you'll thrive as an entrepreneur?
- What character traits might make you struggle as an entrepreneur?
- How do you deal with high-stress situations?
- What's a belief you hold firmly that others disagree with?
- What do you consider "working hard"? How many years do you think you could maintain it?
- What in your past has prepared you to be a startup founder?

Values

Many people have the founder traits, but whether they will mesh well with you is another thing. Earlier in this chapter, you questioned yourself on the factors to ask yourself before going all-in. You also need to decide on your tolerance for working with others with different values. Your morals and what you're prepared to do to succeed can cause conflicts. If one founder bends the truth and the other feels uncomfortable with this, you'll have pent-up resentment. You need to be able to trust and respect each other to last.

Questions to ask

- Who have you most enjoyed working with in the past and why?
- Who have you least enjoyed working with in the past and why?
- What attracts you to me? What doubts do you have?
- What's important to you beyond work? What would you prioritise before the startup?
- What methods are legal but unethical when scaling a startup in your eyes?
- We're going to reach out to people who know you. What do you think they'll say about you?
- Do you have any regrets about the ways you've led in the past?
- How do you deal with conflict?
- What culture do you want for the team?

- How would you pick between two investors offering the same terms?
- What is your working style?

Long-term vision

There's a vast difference between startups and small businesses, and all cofounders need to be on the same page about what they want long-term. You need to know how you define success to attract the right cofounder. There will be arguments when one founder wants to change the world and another wants to get rich fast.

Questions to ask

- Would you rather be the world's greatest lover, but have everyone think you're the world's worst lover? Or would you rather be the world's worst lover, but have everyone think you're the world's greatest lover? [Warren Buffett]
- What does success look like to you?
- What would make you want to step away from the startup?
- Who are your role models? What inspiration do you take from them?
- Do you have any regrets about your path in life so far?
- How would you hope we describe your contribution in 5 years?
- How much equity do you believe would be fair?
- What are your expected cash flow needs?

Complementary skillsets

This is the obvious one. If you're a technical founder and don't know anything about business, find yourself a cofounder who does. You want a team which can build and sell. The skills at the start aren't as critical as what each of you is willing to learn; you want to cover your weaknesses and bits you aren't interested in. The best potential cofounders may be out of your reach. Think about it like football. You can't convince someone at their peak to join your new team. But can you convince them you're the next big thing?

Questions to ask?

- What skills do you bring to the team?
- What are your weaknesses that you hope we'll cover?
- What roles and responsibilities do you think you're best suited to, and why?
- What tasks do you not enjoy but logically see yourself as the best person to do?
- Which skills do you want to develop?

Where to find cofounders

Many cofounders already know each other well before starting a company together, but there are many ways to find your business soulmate.

Close family and friends

The natural place to start is with those whom you know and trust well already. There are many instances of startups founded by siblings, couples, best friends and so on. When this works, it's magic. You spend all your time with the people you love the most. Yet when it goes wrong, it can mess up all areas of your life! You should still assess the fit as cofounders with someone you grew up with because it's a different kind of relationship.

I know of many cofounders hide their relationship status because they worry investors will see it as a risk. Deepak Ravindran and Emilie Vanpoperinghe, cofounders of OddBox, are an exception. The married couple's company has delivered ten million boxes of food that would have otherwise gone to waste.

Acquaintances from school or work

Going a little wider, building with someone you know from a more professional environment can work well. You still have a good understanding of them and can get close references. But the lines between personal and business aren't immediately blurred, and the consequences of something going wrong don't feel as severe. Varun Bhanot and Sunil Jindal worked together at a startup for several years before leaving to found Magic, the fitness mirror powered by AI. Together, they've scaled the company to millions in revenue!

Friends of your network

I love this hack that one of my podcast guests told me. Think about existing leaders whom you respect and have a good relationship with. Ask them who their five smartest friends are who could be open to opportunities. Keep doing this until you meet the right person. Also, secret subtext: if the mutual connection doesn't rate you highly, they won't bother with the introduction. Take the loss and work on improving.

Get yourself out there!

Get yourself to events. Meet people. Do the work. Build a reputation. My organisation, Bae HQ, organises loads of events in London. There are startup communities in major cities all across the world. Go to events with the type of people who would be a potential cofounder. Looking for a technical cofounder? Go to techy events! This is true both online and offline. If you build a personal brand, you'll start attracting potential cofounders who then have a public history to judge you by.

Take part in a programme

There are a bunch of accelerators and incubators designed to match you with a cofounder. For some of these, you need to be a full-time entrepreneur, whereas others are part-time. They have some huge success stories, but you also have to be realistic. Not everyone finds the cofounder they want to stick with through the program. You can also take part in hackathons, which are social startup competitions. Randomly selected teammates can end up being lifelong cofounders.

Cofounder matching platforms

Finding cofounders is a common problem for founders, so unsurprisingly, some entrepreneurs have tried to solve it through tech. You can test out different platforms and see if you strike lucky.

Cold outreach

You can randomly email and message people you find interesting. The challenge, of course, is that you don't have much to offer at the start, and it can seem evasive if you don't give the person much detail of what you want from them. Yet it can and does work.

How to test the relationship

On average, it takes a startup 7 to 10 years to go public. You've got a messy road ahead of you if you choose the wrong cofounders and give them too much power. A warning: I know many founders who publicly seem to love their cofounder, but it's bitter and toxic behind the scenes.

Don't rush

Think of it like a marriage. You want to date and get to know each other before tying the knot. Even if you were friends or colleagues before, this is a new type of relationship.

Ask awkward questions

When you're dating, you want the person sitting opposite you to ask the hard questions which matter to them. What are the dealbreakers? You can use the questions from earlier in this chapter to guide you.

Do your due diligence

Talk to your mutual friends. Find out what they think about them. Ask people who they've worked with before, and let them talk to people you've worked with before. You're going to have a long-term relationship, potentially. It's better for them to find out something they don't like at the start rather than keeping secrets.

Start with small projects

Bae HQ began small with a podcast and pitch deck reviews. Our scope increased over time, which gave my cofounder and me time to shape our relationship slowly. You can build a test project first, where you don't even incorporate a company. Ideally, it's something related to the longer-term plan.

Start on the right track

I'll be honest: this next bit is to do as I say rather than as I did. My cofounder and I have a complex web of interconnected relationships. Neither of us could screw over the other because our reputations would be ruined! We should have had an agreement in place rather than relying on this with hindsight. You want the relationship to be transparent and structured once you're past the testing phase.

It's vital to write everything down and not rely on a verbal agreement over a late-night session. Memory is fallible. It's as simple as sending an email with what you discussed, and your cofounder confirming it's an accurate representation. You can use standard legal templates for a cofounder agreement, though it can be helpful to include a trusted lawyer if either party is uncomfortable. It should include:

- **Roles and responsibilities** - What are your expectations of each other?

- **Equity split and vesting schedule** - Who owns what and how is it earned?

- **Decision-making & conflict resolution** - What happens if you can't agree on a business-critical point?

- **Exit scenarios** - What do you do if one founder wants to leave or is forced to?

Splitting equity between cofounders is a touchy subject. Some cofounders insist they should have a higher share than the others. This makes it clear who is ultimately the boss. I lean toward having as close to an equal split as possible. All cofounders are in it together. Why start a company with someone unless you need them?

You can use vesting and cliffs to protect yourself against bad leavers. These can be complex, but it means cofounders lose some or all their equity if they leave early. The remaining cofounders get the forfeited shares. The greatest rewards go to the founders who stick around the longest. Don't overcomplicate your agreement. Your startup will change over time, and weird clauses add an unnecessary admin burden.

How to maintain the relationship

Signing a cofounder feels like a win, but the work has only begun. You can have the best selection process ever and end up hating each other! Here are a few tips to help make the relationship as smooth as possible:

Blur personal and professional

Personal pressures affect us at work, whether we like to admit it or not. Startup life is high pressure, and you're likely to snap at your cofounder one day when you shouldn't. You can support each other better when you know what's going on in each other's personal lives. My cofounder and I have an unspoken agreement to cover each other whenever we're dealing with family or other personal issues.

Bias toward immediate candour

Don't let any negative feelings fester toward your cofounder. Tell them, respectfully and immediately, so it can be nipped in the bud. A solid relationship needs you to both understand how to break bad news to each other in an effective manner.

Just like a marriage, the worst thing you can do is tell them you hate the way they've been doing something the entire 3 years you've been together. Ignoring minor problems early allows them to grow into big ones down the line.

Regular catch-ups

Setting aside time for deeper discussions away from day-to-day tasks can prevent a relationship from turning sour. It can be easier for some to bring up concerns in what feels like the right setting rather than trying to find the perfect moment.

Celebrate the wins

Cofounders have never-ending to-do lists. You can't only talk to your cofounder about tasks they need to do without appreciating what they've done. Celebratory drinks or dinners when you hit a milestone can go a long way!

Get third-party help

There's no shame in involving trusted third parties when making decisions. You want someone who all the cofounders respect - like someone on the board. You can also get professional help from cofounder coaches, which founders use to great advantage. They can create a safe space for frank discussion.

Parting ways

Cofounders leave businesses all the time, and it doesn't have to be a catastrophe. It's better for a cofounder to leave on good terms than to stay and the relationships get worse. It's possible that their personal circumstances have changed, and they shouldn't have to feel guilty about this. They could stay on as an advisor. Their equity will be adjusted according to your cofounder agreement.

Summary

- Execution is everything in startups, and the cofounding team is the key factor.

- You need bias toward action, unorthodoxy, resourcefulness, resilience, magnetism, focus and self-awareness to get in the founder mindset.

- You'll need to go full-time as a founder to build something world-changing - decide what factors matter for you.

- While you can be successful as a solo founder, it's easier with a good cofounder.

- Use warm introductions wherever possible to find your cofounders.

- Test a cofounder relationship and set out a founder agreement before committing to a cofounder.

- Don't get complacent with cofounders and work hard to maintain a good relationship.

Exercises

- Assess yourself in each area of the founder mindset and identify where you either need to improve or need a cofounder to cover you.

- Write down answers to all the questions about going all-in for your startup - repeat this exercise whenever you need to.

- Decide whether you believe you need a cofounder or not, so you can start passively looking.

- Create lists of potential cofounders from your network and trusted individuals to make recommendations to you.

- If you already have a cofounder, ask them the questions in this chapter to check you're on the same page and review your processes for maintaining your relationship.

Chapter 2

Obsessing over problems and customers

Getting obsessed with your own ideas is a shortcut to failure. You must break this mentality to build anything meaningful. A problem people care about is the foundation of every startup. I've got good news and bad news for you. The bad news is the human race has unlimited problems, and new ones appear every day. The good news is you'll never run out of potential problems to take on. Your challenge is working out which ones have the best potential for you as quickly as you can. We're going to look at how to discover problems, shortlist them, research the customers in-depth, and then decide whether to pursue further.

I know it's tempting to jump to the solution. But you can't build something people want unless you've spent time with them! The only exception is where the solution is derived from legitimate scientific breakthrough research. Startups which begin this way follow an upside-down path, having a solution and trying to find a problem. While we should be thankful to them for furthering human knowledge, it can take these startups years to make money from their invention. You want to avoid the mentality of here's this cool thing I can do with tech - does anyone want it?

Discovering problems

Anyone who tells you that everyone follows the same process to find ideas is a liar. I've interviewed almost 400 founders. There's no one-size-fits-all, so I'm going to run through the different ways you could find a gap worth exploring. Try the methods you like. I encourage you not to run with the first problem which seems interesting because it will probably suck. Nothing personal. The more problems you see, the stronger you'll be at spotting what's high potential.

Work life

If you've ever had a job, you'll know there are processes which feel painful and you wish there were an alternative. This is a spark. Do other people at your company suffer from the same issue? How about those working at your employer's competitors? Be careful about using company time to build your startup idea, as it can get messy with IP rights down the line. You might have a boss who doesn't care, but no harm in being cautious. The enlightened employers will encourage you to strike out on your own! Then you've got your first customer.

Example: Rhim Shah realised financial crime intelligence was far more manual than it needed to be based on his experience at Revolut. He cofounded Arva AI, which is backed by Y-Combinator, to take this on!

Personal life

Unless you live a more charmed life than I, shit happens. What are your greatest frustrations? When have you searched frantically for a solution but not found anything to fill your void? Build a startup to scratch your own itch. Be self-aware enough to know that you might not be representative of your average customer.

Example: Ahana Banerjee is the founder and CEO of Clear. She grew up with skincare issues, so she researched the space in-depth, looking for solutions and spotted the gap. She knew the problem inside out when she started building her app!

Those close to you

Assuming you're not heartless, you've got people around you who you care about. You'll have spent a decent chunk of time listening to their problems. Where have you been stuck when offering advice? When have you wished there was a company to recommend, but you couldn't find anything? Maybe you and the sufferer could be cofounders.

Example: Asesh Sarkar realised financial debt crippled his child's nanny, even once she had a stable, well-paid job. He founded SalaryFinance because he thought there must be a way to support people like her. They've now lent over $1 trillion!

Groups you care about

Beyond your immediate circle, you could have a soft spot for certain groups of people. It could be children, older adults, immigrants, the working-class or any other group. Engaging with the group and listening to them can start to uncover issues you might not even know existed.

Example: Navjot Sawhney travelled to rural India to aid villagers with Engineers Without Borders. He met Divya, who toiled for hours every day manually washing clothes. He invented The Washing Machine Project, which has given hundreds of thousands of people the dignity of clean clothes.

Second-order effects

The news cycle never stops flowing. Think about the asymmetric effect of headlines on different groups of people. At times, new problems which need solving are created, and at others, the intensity dial is turned way up on an existing one. Chaos is a ladder. The PESTLE framework by Francis J. Aguilar is a handy tool to guide you on areas to look at. It stands for Political, Economic, Social, Technological, Legal and Environmental.

Example: Compliance standards are constantly increasing, which triggers the desperate need for secure solutions. Our board member, Jay Gujral, is part of the founding team of Rekord, which uses blockchain technology to give companies peace of mind.

Country arbitrage

Immigrants are classic outsiders and have an edge in spotting problems. They see problems which are solved in one country but not in another. But you don't need to be an immigrant to take advantage of this arbitrage. You could go on holiday and use a product you're shocked you don't have in your home country.

Example: Will Shu lived in New York and loved using DoorDash. He saw an opening in London because there was nothing similar. He founded Deliveroo, which DoorDash eventually agreed to buy for billions.

Industry

Tech adoption varies between industries, especially when you go into sub-niches. The headlines may focus on the biggest issues, which are the most sexy, but this can attract flocks of aspiring founders. An industry which is slow to modernise is a challenge, but there can be greater unexploited opportunities. Where you have a close tie to a sector, you can spot issues which others don't realise exist. You want to target an industry with unhappy customers!

Example: Murvah Iqbal realised delivery was ripe for disruption in the UK with poor customer experience across the industry. She cofounded HIVED, which has delivered millions of parcels and partnered with many household name brands.

Trends

Humans are complaining machines. We complain all the time. Luckily for you, with so many online communities, you can hear about all these problems. Join communities on topics you're considering. See what people ask for help with, and no one seems to have a good answer for them. Look at reviews and testimonials of apps in areas you're interested in too. Zone in on where there's misalignment between what customers need and what current solutions offer. You can check trends too to see whether interest is growing.

Example: Greg Isenberg founded Ideabrowser, which scans the internet using AI for trends and suggests startup ideas every day!

Bonus: Problems while building

I already told you most ideas suck. Yet sometimes you should work on them anyway. Some companies take years to take off, while others have their big break in an unexpected direction. The act of building a company will open your eyes to a whole new world of problems. A problem you experience here could turn out to be a massive opportunity. Check out Chapter 6 for more.

- Slack started as an online video game company.

- YouTube started as a dating platform.

- Instagram started as a check-in app.

- Shopify was a snowboarding company.

- Samsung was a grocery store.

Shortlisting problems

Eventually, you'll have a list of ideas. Some good, some bad and some downright ugly. Now you want to pick a few to deep dive into. We're going to do a basic founder-problem fit test here, which you will update after your research. You might have uncovered a trillion-dollar problem, but if you're not the right person for it, you'll waste time trying to build it.

You'll also want to weed out tar pit ideas. The concept was created by Y-Combinator, and it is where an idea looks good, but you'll get stuck if you jump in. They trigger the "why hasn't someone fixed this?" energy. But there usually is a reason. A textbook one is social media apps or ways to solve loneliness. Everyone is a potential customer! But then you can't get specific enough to be the best solution for anyone.

The Problem Scorecard framework has two elements. The first is the potential of the problem, which breaks down to Intensity, Size & Stickiness. The second is your potential to solve it, which splits into Access, Excitement & Edge. Score each problem out of 5. Rank your ideas in order afterwards. Which problems come out on top? Are you disappointed? Keep ideating if so. You need to trust your gut as an entrepreneur.

The Problem			Your Fit		
Intensity	Size	Stickiness	Access	Excitement	Edge

Intensity

How urgent does this problem feel? You want what investors call a hair-on-fire problem. This is where customers need the solution now! A mild annoyance might be a problem, but will anyone care enough to pay for a solution?

Size

Does the market feel big enough? How many people suffer from this issue? Do they have money? Actual market sizing is more complex, but this is just a gut check. If you're trying to solve a disease which only affects five people in the world, you'll need them to be extremely rich for you to make money. Yet don't discount the adjacent markets. The first problem you solve could be a wedge for further products.

Stickiness

Will this problem still exist in the years to come? The pace of innovation in the AI Age is exciting, but updates from Big Tech have been massacring startups. How do you compete with a goliath that includes your entire startup as a freebie in their existing product? This could be said about any issue. The secret is in being the best in a particular niche, which isn't lucrative enough for the giant companies to go for.

Other risks will mark down the stickiness score, such as platform risk. If your solution is dependent on another company's product, what happens if they increase integration prices? Likewise, if the regulatory environment is uncertain, there's greater risk in going all-in.

Access

Do you know how to reach people with this problem? Will they reply to you? I judge people when they ask me how to find their first customer. Why are you building something where you don't know any potential customers?! You should at least have some idea here; otherwise, you're targeting the wrong group. Can you get started without extremely high costs?

Excitement

Does this problem excite you? Do you want to spend at least 5 years of your life on this problem if all goes well? Here's a secret. I know many "successful" entrepreneurs who are 5 years into a business they no longer care about.

Edge

Do you have an unfair advantage for this problem? Technical expertise, access to networks, or access to funding. You having personally experienced this problem isn't an unfair advantage. That only counts if you're more obsessed than most others. If everyone has this problem and hasn't solved it, why and how will you?

Researching customers

Now, the real work begins. The most critical group in any startup isn't the founders, investors or advisors. You can assemble an elite team and raise disgusting amounts of money. You'll still lose if no one understands the customers' needs. The startup graveyard is full of self-centred founders who thought they knew best. The only feedback which matters is from target customers. Too many founders ask mentors to validate their idea. Talk to your potential customers, then tell mentors you're solving a real problem - don't ask them.

There are different ways to understand the problem space, but nothing beats talking one-to-one with customers. You want to uncover a secret through these conversations, which gives you unique insight. Test the assumptions you have. Interviews are scary for some founders, but if you don't have the guts to talk to customers, then your startup cannot survive. That's our focus here - then I'll share ways to add to this afterwards.

Where to find people

Specificity is your friend in startups. Expect an eye roll if you dare to say everyone is your target customer to an investor. When you talk about target customers, you should have a vision of who you're serving. Pay attention to the following traits:

- **Demographic:** Age, gender, job title, location, marital status, wealth, ethnicity, education level, and so on.

- **Psychographic:** Values, attitudes, habits, lifestyle choices, interests, beliefs, and so on.

If you're unsure what grouping would be most relevant, you can interview several specific customer segments. A marketplace is a unique type of business where you're matching two or more customer segments. Airbnb has two customer segments of renters and rentees, for example. If you're building a marketplace, then interview all segments. When your customers are businesses, then narrow down to the job titles of both the end users and the people in charge of the budgets. Once you're clear on who your customers are, you can find them through:

- Social media and forums.

- Industry events.

- Old colleagues.

- Friends of friends and family.

- Referrals from complementary companies.

- Paid ads.

- Cold outreach.

What not to ask

"The MOM Test" by Rob Fitzpatrick is the gold standard for customer interviews. The core idea is to listen to potential customers rather than tricking them into false positives. Interviewees will lie to protect your feelings or agree with you to avoid conflict. The human tendency to be nice can be devastating for collecting valuable feedback.

You don't want to give any hint of what the solution could be in this phase. If you've got ideas, keep them to yourself. This is all about what the interviewee thinks. You want them to feel comfortable enough to share everything on their mind without trying to please you. Avoid asking leading questions such as:

- Would you use this?

- Is this a good idea?

- Isn't this so annoying?

- Don't you wish someone could fix this?

- How would you solve this?

You're the entrepreneur, not the customer. Don't ask what they want because they don't have the broader perspective you should have. People complaining about how long travelling took in the 1800s would have asked for a faster horse, not a car.

What questions to ask

You want to extract how much the person cares about the problem and whether they're willing to pay. Interviews only need to be 5-15 minutes. Encourage them to talk most of the time. This is about them, not you! Establish the way they currently do things and the intensity of the pain. Tell me more/why/how. You don't need to know the names of their pet rabbits unless you're trying to solve a problem for them! I know it sounds confusing. Here are some valuable questions as a guideline:

- How do you currently do...?
- How do you feel about the process?
- Are there any parts which frustrate you?
- What have you tried to do about it?
- Is it something you think about often?
- How much do you spend on trying to solve this problem at the moment?
- Tell me about the last time you ...
- What workarounds are you using now?
- Do you have any issues with those workarounds?

- What's the most challenging part about this process?

- Why does that matter to your company?

- What solutions are you currently using?

- What's annoying or confusing about them?

- Have you heard of these solutions? Why don't you use them?

Use a note-taking tool or take detailed notes. You want exact quotes which showcase the pain. You know you've struck gold if the interviewee says to you unprompted that they want to buy the solution if you're building it as soon as it's ready! Try to do at least 10 interviews per customer segment or until you're just hearing the same things over and over.

Supporting methods

While 1:1 interviews are the most effective method, you can use these other methods to get a fuller picture.

- **Group interviews:** Organise a dinner or lunch with potential customers.

- **Virtual interviews:** Same as in-person interviews, but harder to build rapport.

- **Informal conversations:** Shorter conversations at events and voice notes.

- **Email survey:** A good way to get lots of responses, but each one is less in-depth than an interview.

I've had 17-year-olds collect 200 survey responses in two days (shoutout Woodford County High School and Mulberry Stepney Green). You're telling me you can't get responses?

Decision time

Now it's time to go back to our scoreboard and go into more depth.

The Problem			Your Fit		
Intensity	Size	Stickiness	Access	Excitement	Edge

Intensity

Do you still believe this is a hair-on-fire problem, after talking to customers? Were your assumptions correct?

Size

How has your perception of the market changed through the research? Do you need to position it in a different way? Is the market growing? How many people suffer from the problem, and how many are willing to pay? You may fall way short of the £100M annual revenue to become a unicorn for venture capital funding. Yet, if you can potentially make millions in the next 2-3 years, you can then create another product line and upsell.

Stickiness

Were your interviewees confident that the problem would affect them for years to come? Could they see a solution on the horizon and were just waiting for a rule change?

Access

If you did at least 10 interviews, you proved you know at least some people. Yet did you find you needed to refine your target further? Do you know enough people in the space to really gain momentum?

Excitement

Did you like talking to the customers about the problem? If you are successful with your startup, you're going to be talking about the problem a lot more. How do you feel about that? Are you still excited? Will you still be excited in 5 years?

Edge

As you talked to customers, did your gut tell you that you could solve this? Did it feel like your experiences gave you something unique that others didn't have?

The transformation

No matter what problem you're trying to solve, ultimately, your solution needs to help the customer achieve a new state. We have three finite resources at a high level: time, energy and money. You should be affecting one of the three:

- **Time**
    - **Save time** - Free up people's day from mundane tasks. Allows faster processes for businesses.

- o **Increase time** - Only possible for health-related companies!

- **Energy**

  - o **Reduce stress** - People will pay to reduce their suffering.

  - o **Increase joy** - Isn't this what life is all about?

- **Money**

  - o **Save money** - Spending a little to save a lot is an easy sell.

  - o **Make money** - Tools which help people increase income or revenue.

You can hit different needs at once, such as helping people make more money and have more fun doing it. Keep whatever goal you're enabling customers to achieve at the front of their minds for everything you do as a company.

Early vs ideal customers

You can identify and categorise your customers better as you get to know them through your interviews and surveys. You may find that people with certain traits have stronger buyer intent than others. These people might not be the highest value segment of your customer base, but they can be early adopters. When you map out the traits of these people, you can build an Early Customer Profile (ECP). You design a fictional person to represent early adopters using demographic and psychographic characteristics. Give them a name. E.g. Nacho. Then every time you make a decision about positioning and what features are essential, you can ask yourself one question. Would Nacho care?

Many consumer startups use students as their early customer persona, such as Tinder and Facebook. The idea is that students are tech-savvy and more willing to experiment than the general population. The segment with the highest potential revenue could be different to the one which creates your momentum. Their traits form the Ideal Customer Profile (ICP). This could be professional segments who have more disposable income, for example.

The danger is ignoring the ECP because you're busy romanticising ICP. Sometimes, the ideal customers may be less willing to test new products and need more traction to believe in you. You can leverage the early adopters for feedback and testimonials until you can get their attention.

Research never ends

Though we're about to progress to building a solution, this doesn't mean the research phase is over! You should always be talking to customers and getting feedback. Stay customer-obsessed and stay ahead of the curve.

Summary

- Obsess over problems and customers, not solution ideas.

- Most ideas suck - use a variety of methods to come up with different problems so you can compare.

- Shortlist ideas with the Problem Scorecard with the criteria of Intensity, Size, Stickiness, Access, Excitement and Edge.

- Focus on direct one-to-one customer interviews when researching customers.

- If you can't find people to interview, you shouldn't work on the problem.

- Ask questions which focus on the problems and customer needs. Seek to understand, not impress.

- Supplement your interviews with surveys, informal conversations, virtual interviews and group interviews.

- Take your problem through the scorecard again now that you have more detail, and see whether it makes sense to pursue.

- Understand what transformation you're giving the customer; are you increasing their time, money or energy or reducing barriers for one of them?

- Separate early and ideal customers and focus your initial effort on the early customers.

- Remember, customer research never ends!

Exercises

- Start tracking potential problems to tackle today. Use notes on your phone or a little black book, but get started.

- Test them using the Problem Scorecard once you have a few you feel strongly about.

- Once you're ready, start doing customer research - you can start by talking to one potential customer.

- Add supplemental research methods.

- Reassess the problem space and decide whether to take it forward.

Chapter 3
Iterating to a solution

When you've done customer research right, the solution creation should be easy. I'm not going to explain the deeper technical side here - you hopefully have someone in your team for that! (If not, find them!) I'm focusing on the process of going from the problem to building something which meets the customer's needs.

Build. Build. Build.

Once upon a time, it took weeks or even months to build a version of your product which could be tested. Now it takes hours or even minutes. The early versions of your product should be as simple as possible. The jargon term for the first messy experiment is your Minimum Viable Product (MVP). Yet the "viable" part is interpreted in inconsistent ways, depending on who you talk to. Nobody serious ever judges you on the quality of your first tries; they judge you on what you learn from them.

I'm going to split between the non-functional MVP and the functional MVP. You can validate with the former and progress to the latter once you believe you have a problem-solution fit. If your team has hyper-efficient builders, then you can skip straight ahead, but the point is not to waste time seeking perfection. All the billion-dollar companies founded by outsiders started somewhere messy.

Non-functional

The simplest of MVPs is a way of validating demand without actually delivering anything. You can create a landing page, which is a simple one-page website where you explain what you're going to do for your customers. The critical part of this exercise is using your customer research to ensure the solution you're selling meets their pain points. You can start with a narrow scope and later widen your net.

You can either ask people to join a waitlist or put a buy button as the call to action on your landing page. The buy button will lead to the waitlist page, too, but it proves the users have buyer intent. A bit of friction in this process can be a tactical decision. If people are willing to push through the inconvenience, then the problem must matter to them. The key is ensuring you can track user behaviour.

You can take payment and deliver the result manually even if the tech backend isn't set up yet. For example, if you plan to build a custom travel itinerary, you can just get everyone's details in a spreadsheet and make the plans yourself. Customers don't care how you do it as long as you meet their needs. Don't try to impress users with how hardworking or intelligent you are.

Functional

Perfection is your enemy. When we say "functional" in the context of MVP, we mean barely functional, held together with chewing gum. Your initial build doesn't need to have the technical basis for the long-term solution. It's your way to get customers and prove traction. Then you get the revenue or the funding for a more scalable build.

The expectations for functional MVPs have increased as AI has decreased building time so dramatically. Yet you have to resist the urge to wait until you've added all the cherries and sprinkles on top of your product. There are many frameworks for deciding what to include. The MoSCoW method by Dai Clegg is a timeless one:

- **Must have** - Non-negotiable, customers have told you they won't use the product unless this is included.

- **Should have** - Important to customers but not a dealbreaker for early adopters.

- **Could have** - Features which some users will like, but most won't even notice.

- **Won't have** - Distractions which you should avoid.

How you categorise tasks needs to be based on what customers care about, not what you think you need. The truth is, you can release your MVP even if it doesn't have some of the Must haves, if you target customers based on the features you have included.

One popular method to avoid bloating the MVP is to set a strict launch date and announce it. Now you can only include what can be ready in time, though pick a deadline in days or weeks, not months or years! If, halfway through, you're feeling shaky about meeting the deadline, then cut fat, don't push back the launch.

Launch. Launch. Launch.

People don't care half as much about your launch as you think they do. Sorry, not sorry. This should free you! You can launch, and it's no big deal if it fails. Then you can launch again. I don't remember any other product launches except maybe the iPad. I thought it was dumb, and later became a customer. Get over your fear of launching and get your MVP out there. The faster you get feedback, the quicker you can bend it to something meaningful.

> "If you are not embarrassed by the first version of your product, you've launched too late."
>
> Reid Hoffman, Cofounder of LinkedIn.

One hack if you're terrified of people judging your product that badly is using a dummy brand and only promoting through anonymous methods. No excuses. You can use techniques from Chapter 4 to help you launch.

Test. Test. Test.

Time to test that resilience we talked about earlier. Customers who give you feedback are doing you a favour. You have to appreciate it and empathise with their concerns. You might disagree, but listen anyway. And it might mean you need to tweak the positioning of the product to attract the right kinds of users.

Pre-user

You might be bracing yourself for comments about minor details, but the feedback starts way before a user actually uses the product.

1. How many people see the landing page link?

2. How many people hit the landing page?

3. How many of them convert?

You've got two drop-off points. Those who don't even click through, and then those who learn more about your product and decide not to continue. Gather as much data as you can about why this is happening. Do people from one source convert more than others? Why do they convert? There are so many signals to help you refine your targeting and positioning.

User

There will be a manageable number of people who actually convert and become your early adopters unless lightning strikes. You can get feedback from the users directly and through tracking the data. You paint a fuller picture of reality when you use both together.

Talk to as many early users as you can. You'll get negative feedback for the early versions of your product if you're doing it right. This is a good thing! The worst result is where users give up on your product but don't bother complaining because they don't care enough. This could show the problem you're trying to solve isn't severe enough. Types of feedback in order of priority:

- **Foundational** - Does this solve the problem? All other feedback is irrelevant unless you're building something people demand.

- **Bugs** - Features which don't work as expected. First, fix the bugs which block a user from knowing whether you can solve their problem. These include security issues, access issues, payment issues and anything else which causes harm to the user.

- **Usability** - Where users can't figure out how to do tasks which should be self-explanatory. You shouldn't need a thick manual for a simple MVP. Jump on calls with users and encourage them to share their screens. Watch what they try to do based on their intent. A feature which can't be found can't solve a user's problem. You can try A/B testing, which means showing alternate versions of the product to different users. You'd then track their experience and conversion.

- **Improvement requests** - These are enhancements which would make the product better for the customer. "I'd be more likely to use this if...". Once you get into improvement requests, you're more on your path to iterating toward the fully featured product. Prioritise these based on the % of users they affect and their importance to these users.

You'll hopefully find the behind-the-scenes data backs up what users are saying. You can also see where users are stopping in processes and try to work backwards to uncover the underlying reason.

You'll want to stay organised throughout the testing phase and keep track of the feedback you receive and your insights from the data. It'll be helpful when you add to your team or need to explain decisions.

Iterate. Iterate. Iterate.

Very few sentences from the first version of this book made it to the copy you're reading. Every chapter in this book has been painfully rewritten, several times over. Chapters have been smushed together and dropped along the way. You can only get to a final product by having a starting point to improve from.

Every major company you admire started from an embarrassing mishmash of an MVP. Your MVP doesn't need to look anything like your final product to serve its purpose. Now the job is to keep updating until one day you're proud of your product. Ship updates as fast and as often as possible. Some day, you'll have enough users where stability becomes essential. Then, you can shift to regular cycles to allow for proper testing and prioritisation of feature requests.

Product-market fit

Your iteration should keep pushing you toward product-market fit (PMF), but be careful about declaring victory prematurely. PMF isn't when you have a few happy customers. PMF is where paying users love your product and depend on it. It's where your systems can't keep up with how fast your usage and demand are growing. You're no longer chasing anything; you're being chased. You'd be mourned if your startup were to disappear. While the product solving the problem is one part, Chapter 5 will dive into the finances. PMF is the signal to start hiring and expanding.

But. But. But.

There are exceptions to this experimental mindset for regulated industries. You can't just test vaccines in such a carefree way for obvious reasons. I'm assuming common sense from you all here!

Summary

- Don't aim for perfection with your solution; aim to solve a painful problem.

- Non-functional MVPs are a way to test whether you have the framing of the problem-solution fit correct and validate demand.

- Functional MVPs are an early version of the actual product, where you can collect customers to iterate from.

- Launch fast, learn, then launch again - you need people to see the product to get meaningful feedback.

- Analyse the funnel to understand who is converting and why.

- Group feedback into foundational, bugs, usability and improvement requests.

- If no one cares enough to use it, then you're on the wrong path.

- Keep iterating the product based on feedback until you reach product-market fit.

Exercises

- Make a landing page for any idea. Learn how easy it is to do so when you do it for your real idea; you have no reason to delay.

- Build a fake app using any AI building tool.

- Start analysing apps you use and landing pages you hit to understand why they are constructed the way they are.

Chapter 4
Earning attention

You can have the best product in the world, but if no one knows it exists, how much revenue will you make? The answer to that is *zero*. Through this chapter, we'll first nail the most vital elements of your brand and your positioning. Then we'll move into strategies and techniques for getting customers to open their wallets.

You should know who your ECP and ICP are from Chapter 2. These are the people you need attention from. Avoid the trap of trying to impress other startup founders harder than to attract potential customers. Otherwise, you can gain fame without revenue. We want your brain to win, not your ego. Too many founders are chasing vanity goals rather than doing their real job. Attention is a means to an end, not the end for real entrepreneurs. Get to the stage where you're overflowing with paying customers, then start giving advice to other startup founders.

Brands aren't forever

Spending time on your brand can be fun, which can catch you off guard. Tinkering with your brand is procrastination from doing the more impactful tasks. The visual elements of your brand and even the name in the early days can be placeholders. I made our original Bae HQ brand assets in a day. I refreshed the brand once we started gaining traction and enough people knew us for it to matter. I had a clearer idea of what our community valued by then. You can change any visual element of your brand, even once you have scale.

You're wasting time trying to come up with the perfect future-proof pixels rather than validating if anyone wants to buy the product. You should make visual elements which are good enough to test and move on. Trillion-dollar companies change their logos, so you have no justification to think yours will be permanent. The exception is if your unique selling point is design, but then you should have the experience to move fast anyway. Tips to make sure your brand doesn't suck:

- **Name:** Easy to spell, not too long, not too similar to a competitor, and domains & social handles available.

- **Logo:** Simple is better, so it can work on many backgrounds.

- **Colour scheme:** Meets accessibility standards.

- **Font:** Readable, professional.

The worst thing you can do is ask amateur friends and family for their opinions. You'll get tonnes of noisy feedback. Wait until your product delivers, then do A/B testing as discussed in Chapter 3. Other elements of your brand don't matter for a long time. Prioritise happy customer testimonials. They'll count for way more than self-proclaiming you're "kind" and "customer-first".

Be the only choice

Your brand positioning matters from day 1 - though it will be iterated on too. You need to use your customer research to place your product as the solution to their problem.

Founders go wrong by using words like leading, best, biggest, better, faster, cheaper and so on. These are all relative to other companies. Forget about the competition. They should be irrelevant. You should be the only logical choice.

You might need to narrow down your niche for this to be true. Can you be the only specialist tool for plumbers rather than just another tax management tool? You could then expand to other tradespeople if you dominate this niche. If there's another player in your niche but you're 10x better than them, you can act as if they don't exist. Bae HQ is "the" community for high-growth Asian-Heritage founders & investors. Not "a", not the "biggest," nor the "best". No one else is your competition to anyone reasonable.

You only have a strategy if you're different from competitors in a way that customers care about. You've done the research. Don't make the mistake of having an insignificant differentiator. If you can't tie back your strategy to direct quotes from customers, then you may need to pause and rethink. Investors will want to know this too.

You look petty if your entire strategy hinges on insulting others in the market. I've lost count of how many 1-person startups claim a billion-dollar company sucks. They claim they can do so much better, but their startup doesn't last a year. Don't do it. Though if you're going to do it, make sure you win. Kit vs Beehiiv is a fun example where the founders have gone toe-to-toe in public. They know where their products shine, and they attract loyal tribes.

Two tests for your positioning:

- **Stupid test** - Do at least some people think your strategy is stupid? This is a good sign, as you can only avoid haters by not doing anything original. Many people considered Airbnb ridiculous when they first pitched the idea.

- **Opposite test** - Would flipping your strategy be irrational? Nobody would market a low-accuracy AI chatbot, for instance. You can only ignore this test if the data backs you up. E.g. Sky brands itself as the UK's fastest broadband.

Hero's journey

How often do you buy a product to support the founders? I'm guessing most of the time, you don't care. You're buying to meet your needs. All your potential customers are the same. They only care about your product if it improves their lives in one of the ways we covered in Chapter 2. The job of your brand is to make this outcome as blatant as possible.

Recall the most effective adverts you've seen. They'll show a character with a problem which you can relate to. You'll feel their pain. Then you'll watch as the company's product solves their issue and they transform. If they were hungry, now they're satiated. Your customer is the hero. I love Slack founder Steven Butterfield's timeless explanation of this - "We don't sell saddles here." What do you think this means? Saddles are a gateway to the joy of horse riding. A saddle advertisement could focus on close-ups of the leather, or it could show someone riding free. How can you use this for your product?

Word of mouth

The dream is to scale because your customers are so delighted that they tell everyone they know to join too. Imagine a stage where users evangelise you, influencers promote you, and the press cover you without you needing to ask. You don't have to hard sell because your potential customers have the fear of missing out.

This flywheel won't spin until you've spent the time and energy working with customers to deliver exceptional value. A key marker of success for Bae HQ is how many people join because their friends told them they had to! "My friends keep going on about you guys" is music to my ears. Leverage positive feedback when you can through case studies, reviews, and testimonials. I read these before buying, and I'm sure you do too! You can encourage customers to post on independent platforms for greater trustworthiness.

A warning. While at the start, you can go above and beyond to convert angry critics into passionate promoters, you can't please everyone forever. You're figuring things out. You'll be tempted to go off track to not lose anyone, but you have to let some go. Focus on your core audience and be upfront about who you can't support to avoid disappointment.

P.S. A positive review of this book from you will make my day.

Network effects

Word of mouth is more critical for some startups than others. Network effects are a powerful tool where the value of your product increases as you gain customers. If your product is eligible, then it can lead to explosive growth once you have the mechanics right. These are the products you see go viral out of nowhere.

- **Direct network effects** - Primarily one type of user, and the more of them, the better. E.g., the more of your friends who use WhatsApp, the more valuable it is for contacting your friends.

- **Indirect network effects** - Two or more types of users which you connect to each other. Marketplaces need users on both sides to have any value. E.g., no one would list on Airbnb if there were no potential renters, but renters will only go to the site if they know there are listings.

Yet companies with network effects can suffer from the cold start problem. Why would anyone join at the start when there's no one for them to connect to? This is where a thoughtful strategy is needed to create localised network effects. Facebook and Tinder both started on a single campus, for example.

Doing things that don't scale

Founders must have their heads in the clouds but their feet on the ground. How you get your first 10 users will be nothing like how you go from 100,000 to 1,000,000. Get your initial customers any way possible. You won't exist long otherwise! Paul Graham coined the term "doing things that don't scale", which explains this perfectly. Here are scrappy ways to get started, which you can't rely on long-term.

Unleash your network

You get limited favours from your friends and family before you become annoying. Use them wisely. I've pissed off people in the past by asking them for favours which weren't relevant to them. I find it works best to ask people who don't have huge networks but have strong trust bonds with a smaller group of people.

Let's say you're launching a product aimed at bankers. It's too much to ask a friend who is in charge of a huge division to send an email to everyone they work with. Yet asking a friend who has a WhatsApp group with a dozen people to share there could lead to a couple of customers. If you had five customers and now you have seven, that's meaningful growth! Save the bigger favours for later on.

Meet them in person

Online presence has much greater scale potential, as you'll see later in this chapter. Yet in-person presence has much greater depth. It allows you to use more tools to persuade someone that you'll solve their problem.

- Go to lots of industry events.

- Hand out leaflets.

- Knock on doors.

- Give out free gifts.

- Leave a lasting impression.

A bit of common sense goes a long way here. If you're targeting fitness fanatics, then join run clubs. If you're targeting foodies, then do short-form interviews with prizes at food festivals. You get the idea. Be anywhere and everywhere until you see results.

Leverage online communities

The quickest way to grow your online presence isn't to start from scratch but to leverage existing communities. You might want users to come to your page. But you need to post where they are, not where you want them to be. There are two key strategies to use:

- **Posting** - Use community-based platforms, which can be anything from dedicated apps, social media groups, and private group chats.
    - **Product promotion** - Some platforms are specifically for founders looking to showcase products, like Product Hunt. These can be a fantastic source of feedback, but you might not be reaching target customers unless you're selling to business owners.
    - **Customer hangouts** - Others aren't for users to promote, and the rules can be stricter. Yet these are where the people experiencing the problem you're trying to solve hang out. Be respectful when posting. Accept the loss if you get kicked out and don't argue with

the moderator. They may be helpful in the future

- **Commenting** - You can also find relevant content on social media and forums, and comment about what you're doing. Add value in the comment so you don't appear to be copy-and-paste spam. Neil Tanna and his cofounders at Howbout did this. They replied to 40,000 comments sharing their tool!

Cold outbound

You should expect a humiliatingly low success rate when reaching out to strangers to try your product. Yet the hustle pays off if you send 1,000 messages and get 10 customers who then tell their friends.

You'll need to humble yourself and get used to being ignored - acting like a spoiled child at rejection gets you nowhere. As long as your message is respectful, most people won't hold an unwanted email against you. This changes if you follow up incessantly. I receive over 100 emails from strangers trying to sell me something every day. I don't have time to reply, nor should I need to tell you why I'm not interested!

Cold outreach through social media channels where you have some social proof is more effective in my experience. When you get new followers, message them all. You might convert someone who was on the fence into a loyal customer. Cold calls and emails make me suspicious, but do what's best for your target demographic.

Exclusivity

Fake exclusivity as a tactic is difficult for outsiders to pull off. You need to have a mountain of hype around you. You may remember startups such as Monzo using this in their initial years. You could only get an account if a member referred you, and even then, you were on a waitlist. This playing hard-to-get tactic worked well to let the company grow without being overwhelmed. We all want what we can't have!

Influencers

This tactic didn't exist until the 2010s, but today, everyone and their grandma is an influencer. You can tap into influencers who can spread the word about your product. Some could accept payment in kind, rather than you needing to use up your limited cash reserves.

Guesting on podcasts and short-form content is underrated. Established podcasts won't want to feature a no-customer founder. Yet many podcasters are desperate for guests and will find value in your story for their audience. If only five people listen, that's five more people who know about you than half an hour before!

Viral stunts

Think outside the box. Do something unexpected. Let your creativity shine and see what happens. Aydan Al-Saad took a camera to the streets of London and began asking people how much they earned. Huge taboo for Londoners. He has grown a vast audience, which has enabled him to secure funding for his startup, Skillstore, in a short time.

Do things that scale

You should do things that don't scale for as long as you can. But trust me, I understand that it can become exhausting. I've given up on managing my inbox, and much more of my time is dedicated to things that scale, like writing this book. Scalable growth strategies are where the amount of effort doesn't escalate with the potential returns.

Unscalable strategies can scale with the right systems. Take being a founder who replies to customers personally. You'll feel awesome with 10 customers, strained with 1,000 customers and burnt out with 1 million customers. The reality is, most founders you think are replying have delegated it to their team to pretend to be them!

Content

Platforms and algorithms will change with the weather, so I'm going to focus on the fundamentals here. You can't have missed how many startups are trying to take over your feed.

If the algorithm has realised you're into startups at all, you've probably been bombarded with posts about the importance of personal brand. The general concept is that people connect with people, not companies. Personal brands tend to grow faster than business brands. There's a catch, and it's not so simple. The end goal of content marketing isn't to have a large number of followers but to convert the viewers into paying customers.

- Thousands of startups made millions last year.

- Thousands of startups raised millions last year.

- Thousands of people have become billionaires.

- Thousands of people have built billion-dollar startups.

You can't name 99% of them. You probably can't name the top 10 most followed founders in your space. You don't need a personal brand to win - it's simply a tool which some founders have used to powerful effect.

You can break down content into two major categories with distinct intentions. Discovery content is your top-of-the-funnel, which has a broad reach but doesn't necessarily establish strong brand trust. You use discovery content so people hear about you and then try to move them down the funnel. Deep content is all about trust and loyalty. You get potential and existing customers to spend more time with your brand and increase the likelihood of spending with you.

- **Discovery:** short-form videos, short-form written content, single images, carousels, and disappearing content.

- **Deep:** Podcasts, long-form videos, long-form written content (blogs, research papers), books, and newsletters.

Both types of content are always more time-consuming than expected. You shouldn't start a podcast because your friends think you should. You have to understand how it will help you achieve your goals. The effort-reward ratio is often low, and it can be an expensive distraction. As someone who straddles both spheres, founders underestimate the work of content creators and content creators underestimate the work of a startup founder.

SEO/GEO

Let's define these terms:

- **SEO** (Search engine optimisation) = Rank high on search engine result pages to drive traffic to your website.

- **GEO** (Generative engine optimisation) = Be recommended by generative AI search tools and platforms that reference or cite your brand.

SEO takes a few months to start working, as search engines begin to trust your domain. While the algorithms change, SEO is well understood, and you can follow one of the many guides online to set it up.

GEO, at the time of writing, is a much newer field and is likely to change significantly. Yet there is already anecdotal evidence of startups using it to their advantage. Keep track of updates in this area to take advantage if it makes sense for you.

Ads

When done correctly, paid ads are a repeatable and reliable way to make a return. You'll learn about the LTV/CAC ratio in the next chapter, and a high ratio is crucial for this strategy. When done without being optimised, they can be a way to lose money fast!

Clean up

Getting the basics right for your brand often outperforms trying to be exceptional. You can confuse potential customers if iterations and pivots lead to inconsistent positioning. Keep a checklist of everywhere your brand exists and update each place when needed. Once you have a team, make sure their explanation of your product aligns with the value proposition.

Don't try to do every distribution channel at once. Track your experiments and double down when you get positive signals. Many startups use just one or two channels ruthlessly until they reach over a million in revenue. You need to understand where your customers are and focus your efforts there.

A common mistake for outsider founders is to list a dozen features when trying to explain their product. No one cares about feature 12. From your customer research, you should know the most demanded features, and they should be front and centre across every channel.

The best way to prove you have a clear brand is to ask a customer to explain the product to a friend. If they can't do it, then you need to be clearer. I love asking community members to explain what Bae HQ does. It's a great way of seeing whether the message I'm sending out is working!

Press

I want the press to cover this book, so I'm going to whisper this next lesson. Press coverage is much less important than it was pre-social media boom. Today, many influencers have more engaged audiences than major brand tech outlets. It's a funny world because you might get more views on your social media post about your appearance than the original gets.

Yet perception matters. Being featured regularly by respected organisations and media outlets gives you weight and credibility. Press mentions may sway potential customers who are on the fence about whether to trust you.

The best way to get covered is to be worth covering! Journalists won't care about your startup unless you can show them you're a compelling story for their audience. They don't owe you any favours. Why would a stranger care about your story? Building relationships with journalists isn't as inaccessible as you might think. Their job is to discover interesting stories, so they want pitches. Before pitching them, understand what kind of story you're suggesting and align it with what their audience wants:

- **Human-centred** - This is about your personal story. Have you overcome remarkable circumstances? Are you an underdog that the public can get behind? Your story should be uncluttered and straightforward to follow to be enticing.

- **Authority-centred** - Does your domain expertise mean your opinion is valuable to the public? Pay attention to awareness campaigns or when your topic is prominent in the news. E.g., you run a breast cancer detection startup and it's Breast Cancer Awareness Month.

- **Startup-centred** - You've achieved a significant milestone such as closing a major funding round, hitting a revenue target or releasing a world-first technological innovation.

- **Stunt-centred** - You run a marketing campaign which draws significant attention organically due to the shock factor. This can backfire horribly, of course.

- **Scandal-centred** - Hopefully you're on the right side of the controversy! If your startup is fighting against unfair practices in your industry, then you can position yourself as the saviour. People love reading about a scandal!

Press coverage can snowball because once you're recognised and trusted among journalists, they'll keep coming back to you. The RSVP formula in Chapter 8 will be helpful for you.

Summary

- Don't sweat the small details of your brand - these can all change later.

- Focus on your positioning instead, and how to be the only solution for a particular problem and customer segment.

- Use the hero's journey to ensure you focus on outcomes, not features

- Build everything with word of mouth in mind as the most potent growth channel.

- Identify whether network effects are relevant for your product and plot a strategy to overcome the cold start problem.

- Start by doing things that don't scale: unleashing your network, meeting customers in person, leveraging online communities, influencers, cold outbound, exclusivity and viral stunts.

- Mature into doing things that scale: content, ads and SEO/GEO. And build systems for things that initially didn't scale.

- Regularly clean up your brand whenever you pivot to avoid confusing potential customers.

- Craft a story first before worrying about press - they'll come to you if you have a story worth covering!

Exercises

- Create the visual elements of a dummy brand fast - use examples of the original looks of companies you admire to lower your standards.

- Look at brands you love and understand how they position themselves effectively, then test with your own ideas.

- Craft a hero's journey for your ideas.

- Start assessing different tactics you could use to attract your first customers so you can hit the ground running.

- Decide whether you'd like to go down the content route.

- Keep track of wherever you want your brand to live.

- Start following journalists on social media in your problem space!

Chapter 5
Managing finances

You can be obsessed with the problem and create a brilliant product. But you have to keep your startup alive for any of your bold visions to come true. Startups die when they run out of money ("runway" in investor jargon), so your job is to make sure this doesn't happen!

I make it sound simple, but we've had months where I've had to borrow in an emergency to pay our team. I've got overexcited about potential income and nearly lost everything. The timings of comings and goings are crucial to your survival. Bae HQ closed huge deals in the same month that we almost went bankrupt. The terms on those payments meant they wouldn't arrive for 30 days, and we had to cover costs somehow in the meantime. Understanding this crunch is critical, and you must keep a sharp eye on your bank balance at all times.

Broke entrepreneurs can maintain inauthentic personal brands where you think they're doing so well. In reality, they could be one delayed payment away from being evicted. Block out the noise. If you know you have no money, then don't let awards and achievements get to your head. You don't have a business without money.

Bootstrapping

Your default path should be building without taking external capital. This gives you complete control of the company. If you can scale fast this way, then all eventual profit is yours! There are three ways to bootstrap:

- **Savings** - Putting your own money into the company to get it going in the hope you can pay yourself back later. (Only works if already wealthy!)

- **Pre-sales** - You can announce your planned product and start collecting revenue before you've even delivered. This works best in consumer goods, but can work in other industries too.

- **Early revenue** - Actually making sales and delivering with good margins so you can reinvest the money back into the business.

I've seen many former bankers and consultants put six figures plus of their own money to get their company off the ground. I put in tens of thousands myself to get Bae HQ started. This option might not be available to you, and you'll need to be more resourceful.

Startup business models are designed for scale, yet you can make money faster through old-school methods. You could do consulting and advisory work on the side. You could pick up work through the gig economy. It's not uncommon for people to take contracting work at their old company to ease the transition. Depending on what you do, you can use it to build relationships at the same time. I know someone who drives an Uber around major tech conferences and meets investors and VIPs!

While owning the whole company sounds great, there are obvious risks. If the company doesn't work out, then your savings are lost. If your competitors have more capital, it can be hard to compete with their growth. Some startups by nature need heavy capital investment on day one - for instance, you can't build a contagious diseases lab in your kitchen! You may also be forced to think short-term because you have no runway. External capital can come with extra mentoring and advice, which you'd find valuable too. Finding imperfect ways to keep cash flowing when you go into these conversations can give you leverage. The other side knows you *want* to raise rather than that you *need* to raise. The less desperate you seem, the more interested people are - just like dating.

Maximising revenue over profit

Wrapping your head around startup finances can be counterintuitive. Most businesses focus on maximising profits, like Economics 101 teaches. Yet startups are revenue-obsessed. When founders talk about growth, they're talking about revenue, not profit. They can brag about growing 100% year-on-year and being on track to hit £100M revenue while spending twice as much as they make.

The method to the madness is that if the startup can dominate a niche, they can later improve margins or increase prices. It's a long game where the payoff can be incredible. Take a look at how long it took these household names to become cashflow positive:

- Facebook = 5 years.

- Amazon = 9 years.

- Uber = 15 years.

- Spotify = 18 years.

External funding kept them alive long enough to make shareholders extraordinary returns. Yet these types of bets are usually made in Zero-Interest Rate Policy conditions. This is where institutions can borrow at discounted rates, which encourages them to take bigger bets. The scrutiny is more intense when interest rates are higher, as investors have a greater opportunity cost. They can get a decent return on safer asset classes, so they'll need much more convincing to invest in high-risk startups.

Insiders know something outsiders don't. You can raise millions and fail miserably. The VC Power Law works on the assumption that most startups a fund backs will fail, but a few outliers will generate extraordinary returns to make up for the rest. Don't let your bank account full of other people's money get to your head. You're accountable for it all. The end goal of external funding is to increase your runway to give you more time to become profitable. If you go through the venture rounds, the point of each round is to give you time to gain the traction you need for the next. You'll be far more attractive to acquire if you're not losing money every month!

Customers > users

Let's make a distinction between users and customers. Users use your product (duh!) but don't necessarily pay. Customers are the paying users of your product. You want to convert users to customers as soon as you can. History is full of examples of startups making previously free features paid and having to back down because of user outrage.

There are exceptional circumstances where delaying revenue is a smart move. We covered network effects in Chapter 4. When the value of your product is dependent on how many others use the platform, then it can be beneficial not to add any friction for as long as you can afford to. Following a user maximisation strategy is risky but can pay off. WhatsApp had revenue of just $10m when it was acquired for $21bn because of the gigantic size of the user base. As we mentioned before, feedback from paying customers is worth 100x that of users. Without a path to revenue, you don't have a startup: you have an expensive hobby.

Metrics that matter

You don't need to overcomplicate your finances. Keep track of a few key numbers and get professional help when it comes to tax season. It shouldn't be too difficult, unless you're spending money in a million different directions, which you aren't doing, right?

Essential for all startups:

- **Bank balance** - No BS. How much cash is in your account right now?

- **Recurring monthly expenses** - The total of subscriptions, salaries, contractor fees and other predictable costs which come out of your account each month.

- **Expected expenses this month** - You'll find out as a founder that there are always extra costs which pop up uninvited. You must keep track of these so you know what will be in your account at the end of the month, assuming no revenue. The longer you're in business, the further out you should map this.

- **Burn rate** - Average expected monthly expenses - average expected monthly revenue.

- **Runway** - Total available cash/Burn Rate. This can be close to zero for your first few months! Once you gain funding of some kind, you can start thinking longer term. Until then, it's figuring out how to stay alive!

- **Default alive** - Will you become profitable before your runway ends? Effectively, meaning you never need to raise again.

Business model dependent:

- **Customer Acquisition Cost (CAC)** - How much do you spend through different channels to get a paying customer?

- **Lifetime Customer Value (LTV)** - What is the total expected value of each customer?

- **Net Revenue (NR)** - Revenue minus discounts and returns.

- **User Retention (UR)** - The proportion of paying users in the last period who bought in the current period.

- **Monthly Recurring Revenue (MRR)** - What is the value of the subscription revenue?

- **Net Revenue Retention (NRR)** - What % of last month's recurring revenue do you expect to keep this month, accounting for churn (cancellations)?

- **Gross Margin (GM)** - How much money do you make per sale after taking out the cost of goods sold?

- **Gross Merchandise Value (GMV)** - the total monetary value of all goods and services you sell.

- **Gross Transactional Value (GTV)** - the total monetary value of all transactions you process.

- **Average Contract Value (ACV)** - What is the value of contracts closed on average per year?

- **Monthly Active Users (MAU)** - How many users actually use the app each month.

You can use qualitative metrics, such as surveys and Net Promoter Scores, to assess customer satisfaction. Think of these as early indicators of retention and churn. Low survey scores could show up later as subscriptions are cancelled, and you'll want to act fast. Knowing your numbers gives you and potential investors peace of mind!

Business models

You'd be surprised how long it takes some startups to figure out how to make money. These founders take obsessions with problems and customers too far! Your business model can be changed, and your pricing isn't permanent. You'll probably undercharge to start before you build confidence. Pick your business model based on customer needs and the competitive landscape. Here are some examples with the relevant metrics from the previous section in brackets.

- **Subscription** - You charge a standardised fee at a regular cadence to provide products or services. E.g. Content platforms. [MRR, Growth Rate, NRR, LTV, CAC]

- **SaaS (Software as a service)** - Subcategory of subscriptions where the product is delivered through the cloud and marginal costs are minimal. E.g. Business tool software. [MRR, Growth Rate, NRR, LTV, CAC]

- **Enterprise** - You have bespoke pricing for large organisations, and contract sizes are significant. E.g. CRM platforms. [ACV, Revenue]

- **Pay-as-you-go** - You charge customers based on what they consume rather than a set amount. E.g. cloud providers. [Revenue, NRR, Gross Margin]

- **Advertising** - You charge advertisers for access to your user base. E.g. social media apps. [MAU, UR, CPM, CPC]

- **Transactional** - You enable transactions and take a fee. E.g. payment providers. [GTV, NR, UR, LTV, CAC]

- **Marketplaces** - You link two or more user groups and take a fee when they interact. E.g. Restaurant directories. [GMV, NR, UR]

- **E-commerce** - You sell products online directly to consumers. E.g. consumer hardware. [Revenue, LTV, CAC, GM]

- **Razor and Blade** - You sell initial items at low cost, then sell add-ons. E.g. online games. [Revenue, MRR, LTV, CAC, GM]

- **Deeptech/Biotech** - Specialist business models which most resemble enterprise business models, but can be extremely long-term.

Breakdown of costs

A safe assumption is that everything you try to do will cost more than you expect. Add a buffer to stay alive!

You

You might feel funny being labelled a cost. Don't take it personally, I'm sure you're cool. Yet you need to be paid someday, so you're a cost, especially if you need a salary straight away.

I worked for years on Bae HQ before paying myself. While I don't wear this as a badge of honour, you should realise this is common for startup founders. You're the cheapest resource at the beginning. The trade-off we make is current income for the potential big wins down the road. You must make use of your energy for as long as you can. You're tech, sales, marketing, support, finance, partnerships, operations and any other division you can think of. Do you remember when I told you the journey is easier with cofounders? Does it make more sense now?

Paying yourselves is a contentious topic. It can and has caused friction between otherwise agreeable cofounders. Circumstances change, and lives diverge. How you handle the pressure each other are feeling can determine whether your partnership survives. You've got two options:

1. Little as possible for as long as possible.

2. Enough to avoid personal financial stress.

You might want to be the martyr and go for option 1. It will work for some of you. I've been there and I suffer from the consequences today! You are less effective as a founder if you're distracted by worrying about your personal finances. The earlier you can start paying yourself, the healthier the longevity of your business. Your cost base is artificially low when founders aren't paying themselves market rate. Some day you don't want to do every job, so start tracking the value of the work you're doing so you'll know what it'll cost later.

From an individual founder's perspective, this is your opportunity cost. You're doing jobs which you'd be paid considerable money for elsewhere for free for your startup. Over time, you can become anxious about what you're missing out on - and your significant other may be too! Don't ignore this because one day it could reach a tipping point and you take it out on your cofounders, investors or customers.

Employees

You used to be judged by how many employees you had. You must be doing well to have 50 employees! Times have changed. Revenue per employee has become a more significant metric amongst investors in the age of AI. Yet many incredible founders say they couldn't have got to where they are without their team. Employees who are fully dedicated to your mission can make priceless contributions when the time is right.

Hire full-time employees only when 100% needed. Salaries are often the largest expense for early-stage startups. Spending too much is usually because of overhiring. Yes, they increase your capacity, but they introduce new challenges too. You have to manage them effectively, which takes time away from other founder tasks. Full-time employees are more expensive than their salary alone. Remember to take into account taxes, insurance, benefits, training costs and other expenses. You may need to provide them with equipment and office space. You want to have enough certainty in jobs to be done and revenue to support growth and stay as lean as possible until then. You gain the existential dread of missing payroll, which will cost you many nights of sleep if you're not careful. This might all sound scary, but in Chapter 9, we'll talk about how to hire the dream team.

Outsourcing

The other way to increase your capacity without committing to full-time employees is by using freelancers. When you've got cash flow uncertainty, this is a better option because freelancers give up stability for flexibility. While it's easy to say fire fast, it's tough in practice to let go of an employee compared to not renewing a freelance contract.

Outsourcing non-core work, which is repetitive, is a no-brainer as soon as you can afford it. Outsourcing more highly skilled work is more contentious. You don't want to be reliant on external developers to build your product, who can then hold you hostage. You'll want strong recommendations when using contractors for anything mission-critical to your business.

Advisors

External experts have the potential to prevent you from making mistakes and increase your chances of winning. Founders who already have significant wealth can pay for advisors early on to accelerate their learning. This gives them a competitive edge! Yet they can also be a complete waste of money. Many outsiders can rely on free programmes and networking with fellow founders first.

Avoid any advisors who use pressure tactics to persuade you to become a client!

Always carry out due diligence with an advisor's previous clients before hiring them. It's preferable to have a small circle of advisors whom you trust, rather than too many voices competing for your ear.

Tech costs

The costs for all the tools and software you use in your startup can stack up if you're not paying attention. There are two major buckets:

- **Product delivery** - Tools needed for your product to run, such as web hosting, APIs, payment processors & dev tools. You need to be sure you're getting the best deal here and prioritising what delivers value for the customers.

- **Project delivery** - Tools for the founders and team to work together effectively, such as CRM, messaging, booking services and email providers. These are generally cheaper, but £10 here and there each month can add up over the year.

Some tips to reduce your tech spend:

- Don't pay full price for subscriptions where you can. Many companies offer startup credits. It's not out of the kindness of their hearts. They think once you're locked into a workflow, you won't change and eventually pay full price.

- When you sign up for discounted rates, make sure you budget the full price later down the line. Pay more now if needed to avoid creating an unaffordable liability later.

- Audit your tech tools regularly to see if you're still getting value. Cancel liberally.

- Only sign up for annual subscriptions when you're 100% confident it's going to be the tool you use in a year. Otherwise, you take the financial hit all up front and don't get full usage.

Office space

Insiders and outsiders perceive having an office in opposing ways. Your mates might see a new office as a signal of success and congratulate you. Insiders will see it as excessive spending and judge you. You don't need your own office to be legitimate, and many meetings take place online and in cafes.

The most significant factor to consider is what environment makes you most productive and whether the cost trade-off is worth it. I hate working from home because the temptation to nap or lie down is too great. I struggle working from cafes, because I will react to every sound and movement around me. Our office, at the time of writing, is large but significantly cheaper than one would expect because we're in a basement with an odd-shaped room.

You can tap into the global talent pool to greater effect when you're not tied to an office-first culture. You can save money through hiring where highly-skilled people are available for lower salaries.

Customer acquisition costs (CAC)

Most marketing costs, such as the internal tools and any outsourced help, are covered in other areas. Yet, you should label them as part of customer acquisition separately to accurately calculate your CAC. Sublabelling by distribution channel is critical for understanding where you are getting the most bang for your buck.

Paid ads are an easily trackable cost once you begin using them. So are event ticket costs and related expenses. As you learned in Chapter 4, be as scrappy as you can at first to keep this low. Do the obvious here. Spend the most money on the channels which give the highest LTV/CAC ratio.

Not enough people discuss the competing forces for customer acquisition costs with scale. The more customers you have, the more data you have and the more effectively you can spend your money. But conversely, you gain the easiest customers to convert first, so you have to work harder for later customers, too. This is where having enough people who feel the problem you're solving intensely becomes increasingly evident.

Legal, compliance, and taxes

Urgh. No one likes paying legal and license fees, but they're a necessary evil. The peace of mind is worth it. Likewise, don't forget to budget for taxes. In the UK, you need to pay attention in all directions. It's easy to be hit with a painful fine for missing a deadline for a payment you didn't realise you had to make! Ensure you're using qualified professionals whom you trust.

Opening the floodgates

You should always keep track of your costs and be prudent. Yet the game changes once you hit PMF (Chapter 3). Your costs shouldn't be growing at the same pace as your revenue, and your margins should be improving. When you know you can scale fast with good margins, then it's silly not to spend more!

Summary

- You can bootstrap your company through savings, pre-sales and early revenue to avoid needing external capital.

- Maximising revenue in the early days can be necessary to build the scale for the economics of your startup to make sense and to outcompete.

- Optimise for paying customers rather than users unless network effects are vital to your product and you're being bankrolled by encouraging investors.

- Experiment with business models to find what works best for your product - you may combine several to gain the greatest returns as long as it's not a distraction.

- Learn the key numbers which matter for your business models and make sure you're tracking them regularly.

- Founders are the cheapest resource to begin with, but you must plan for eventually paying yourself well and managing alignment between cofounders.

- Employees are more expensive than simply their salary, and don't hire until you're sure you have the business to sustain salaries.

- Freelancers and agencies are a cheaper and more flexible option to start with, but be careful when using them for anything mission-critical.

- Be wary of spending on advisors rather than doing the work yourself

- Find the best tech tools for what you need and be mindful not to overspend by taking advantage of discounts.

- Track your customer acquisition costs early so you know what's working and what isn't.

- Don't forget to account for service costs to keep ahead of the law and tax authorities.

- Once you have a repeatable and profitable way to scale, don't be afraid to spend!

Exercises

- Brainstorm ways to make money before your product hits scale to reduce reliance on savings and external funding.

- Master the basic financial terms and create a dashboard for yourself to review weekly.

- Plan for what costs your business will need at different stages.

- Set milestones where you won't consider certain costs until they're hit, e.g. we won't pay for an office until it's less than 20% of our revenue.

- Start engaging with service providers to find someone you trust who can take your business forward.

Chapter 6
Staying on and going off track

The first period of your startup is the honeymoon phase. Everything is new. Everything is exciting. Everyone congratulates you on taking the leap. Yet sooner or later, you realise how much work there is to do. Unless you're superhuman, you're going to have moments of feeling lost and wondering whether you should give up. There's a sweet spot of persistence which is unique to every founder-problem combination.

I can't and won't give you a paint-by-numbers roadmap of milestones and dates to hit. Instead, I'm going to provide you with tools to manage your time and direction.

Setting a long-term vision

> "Put a computer on every desk and in every home" – Microsoft.
> "Enable human exploration and settlement of Mars" – SpaceX.

Microsoft's statement sounded crazy when they announced it. SpaceX's statement seems impossible as I write this, but they may have achieved it by the time you're reading. When you're innovating at a globally consequential level, you can set a Big Hairy Audacious Goal (BHAG). Others will think you're crazy, but your team will be inspired by creating generational change. Your long-term vision sets a clear long-term goal to focus your efforts. It reminds you why you bother on the hard days.

North Star metrics are related to BHAGs and are used interchangeably by many people. North Star metrics have a number attached, which allows you to know decisively how close you are. An absolute number is best. For example, a North Star metric for Bae HQ could be for our programme alumni to reach £1 billion in revenue. This won't happen anytime soon, but it gives me something to focus on beyond the daily fires we put out.

Short-term targets

You get the long-term vision sorted first because it then helps you decide on the short-term targets. This top-down approach stops you from building something which you end up not caring about. Yet startup reality means your long-term vision will probably change a few times until you get something which works.

In most cases, your target should be revenue growth in the short term. The faster you scale, the sooner the BHAG seems possible. The problem with a single target of revenue is how easily you can game it. A secondary metric can keep you honest:

- **Reducing CAC/overheads** - There's a graveyard full of startups that made some money but spent much more!

- **Churn and Retention** - You can be incredible on the sales side and keep bringing in new revenue. Yet you might have a leaky bucket where too many customers are unhappy and don't renew. This gives you a false sense of growth, as eventually the bad experiences of churned customers will turn off new customers.

You might find yourself in a more acute situation where you need to flip the primary and secondary metrics. There's no point in chasing revenue targets if you're haemorrhaging money or creating a legion of haters. Fix the most urgent issue first.

You can use the Objective Key Results system, designed by former Intel CEO Andy Grove. Over a set period, you set an objective which has expected results attached to it. You put down the failable tasks to get you there and assign the tasks to someone. At the end of the period, you assess whether you hit the target and the reason for any difference. The objective must be on the path to your North Star and have strategic importance.

Resist the urge to have a million targets because you'll miss most and get demoralised. You can have a scorecard with 5-15 key performance indicators, which act as your overview of how well the business is performing. Hint: you won't need 15 until you hit serious traction. Avoid vanity metrics, such as social media followers or awards, like the plague.

Preventing overwhelm

You'll become your own worst enemy if you're not careful. No one can force you to do anything. Only you can control your time. There will always be consequences for the balls you choose to drop, and you need to know which ones are acceptable for you.

You should spend as much of your time as possible on high-leverage tasks which move you toward your short and long-term goals. You'll sharpen your gut instinct of expected return on time spent on different tasks. Customer obsession has to be at the heart of everything you do. Focus on what makes more people pay for your product and increases retention. Over-optimising minor details, which no one cares about, is procrastination.

I know way too many "multi-award-winning" entrepreneurs who are crashing. They're too busy playing founder publicly, rather than doing the crucial activities behind the scenes, like getting customers. Impressing people who aren't going to buy your product or invest in your startup is a poor use of your time. I intentionally set the bar high for podcast guests on our platform. I want the people who've done the thing and want to give back, rather than those who love the attention. I'm being harsh to make a point. If you never have time for the high-leverage tasks, make sure it's not because you're chasing too many trophies.

Another common mistake is overcomplicating systems when there's no need to. You don't need to reinvent every wheel. Innovators can try too hard to do every little thing in a unique way when it's actually irrelevant to customers. Use standard contracts and processes in most areas of your business and be selective about where you want to differentiate. Here are some simple frameworks to help you:

- **If-then plans** - Don't add a project to your plate until a previous one is in a good state. One example when it comes to distribution channels is "if we're posting every day on platform X and it takes us less than 3 hours a week, then we can start posting on platform Y."

- **Not-do-lists** - Do a brain dump of everything on your mind. Put all the minor tasks on a list of things you aren't going to do. Don't let these take up any of your brain space until your to-do list has space.

- **Done lists** - Keep track of everything you've done during a day. To-do lists can be overwhelming, and it's pleasant to look back on what you've already achieved.

- **80/20 rule** - Prioritise the 20% of factors which produce 80% of the results based on the Pareto Principle. This means being okay with ignoring tasks which have only a small impact, which can sometimes be easier said than done.

Iterating and pivoting

You're going to fuck up. No founder is perfect. You'll make lots of iterations along the way, and this is part of the process. Sometimes, though, you have to face reality where your startup isn't clicking. You need drastic changes.

Pivots are more substantial than iterations when one or more of the core fundamentals of your startup need to change. You might cling on too long before committing to a pivot because you're worried about what other people will think. Yet pivots are normal for startups. Investors will understand, though they may be less interested if you no longer fit into their thesis. Your startup is your entire life, but most others won't care half as much as you might think they do.

You'll realise I was deluded if you go back to the early podcasts of Bae HQ or my early LinkedIn posts. I had the best of intentions, but I had to adapt when some of my assumptions were wrong. I'm sure some people bear a grudge. You can't postpone a pivot because you're worried about upsetting a small number of existing customers. You'll never be able to please everyone. You've got to do what's best for business in the long term. Pivots are behind most of the greatest startups of all time.

Signals to pivot

A single bad day isn't a reason to pivot! Meaningful problem-solving can take a while to hit a tipping point. You might be having a lot of fun, and the business outcomes are less important to you. You might care so much about the problem that you'll find a way to solve it even if it's not necessarily a startup. Here are some signals to look for that it's time to pivot:

Burnout

Are you still excited to work on the problem you chose? Do you have that sinking feeling in your gut all the time? This is more common than you think, but founders don't want to be judged, so they don't talk about it publicly. You'll be outcompeted easily when your heart isn't in it. You only get one life, don't waste it on building something you don't care about anymore.

Headturning

You might not actively resent the startup you're building, but you might be finding yourself spending all your time researching other ideas. I've seen this a lot with founders who become obsessed with healthtech after becoming unhealthy and unfit after their first startups. When your obsession has shifted, maybe it's time for your startup to shift too.

Customers don't care

Customers can dry up after the initial buzz because there are just not that many people who want your solution. You can keep trying to force it, but if you're solving a real problem, customers should be engaging and recommending you to more people. If the product stopped working for a week, would anyone notice? A key red flag is high churn on a subscription product. Sometimes this isn't your fault at all. A new technology or process has emerged which makes what you've built inferior. Look at how many startups have been destroyed by the big AI companies eating their pie.

Team struggles

Many highly qualified people are in roles they hate. If you're hiring and you can't convince any of these people to join you, then you've got a problem. It means they'd rather stay unhappy where they are than join you. Ouch. When you already have employees, you should be able to tell from their engagement whether there's any real excitement. Do they engage with you? Do they ask questions? Do they celebrate company wins? When they're checked out, maybe you should too.

Investors not biting

Rejection is a standard part of trying to raise capital. Some major success stories faced 100+ rejections before getting their first check. You've got to prove them wrong with traction. If you can't, then they could be right.

Stagnation

You're not getting clear signs. You're feeling stressed but not burnt out. Some customers are giving good feedback. Some investors are backing you. But it's all meh. You always seem to be one week away from your big break. You're rapidly becoming a zombie. You're stuck but feel like it's not bad enough to stop. If you're even asking that question, it could be better to nip it in the bud.

7 ways to pivot

1. Customer segment pivot

This is where you realise the solution you've built is great, but the customers you're targeting aren't actually the ideal customer profile. This can be caused by personal biases where you think one group cares deeply about a problem, but other groups are using the product way more. This could also be the case with geographies where your product takes off in one country due to unique circumstances.

2. Problem pivot

This is where the assumption of a key problem for a customer group is wrong, and another issue is much more hair on fire. You can shift your build to focus on solving this problem, instead of staying on a path with more resistance.

3. Product pivot

Maybe you've invested time into building a solution to a problem, and you're getting lukewarm feedback. What you've built isn't really solving their problem. Sometimes, it's best to drop the ego and scrap the product and rebuild. This is hard where the product is good enough for some, but lacks the features which make it a no-brainer for your customers. In the age of AI, with new technological advancements, you can solve the problem in a much more effective way, and it makes sense to restart.

4. Feature-as-product pivot

This happens more than people might think. You're super obsessed with how cool your tech is, but what you thought was a minor feature becomes the most used part of your product. In this case, talking to your users and finding out what makes it so compelling can help you determine whether you should shift your focus to this feature and make it the primary product. You can tell this through tracking usage and reviews and spotting trends.

5. Internal to external pivot

You might not have enough customers who care about your product, but to build it, you've created systems which other businesses could benefit from. The classic example is Slack, which started as a video game, and the tool used for developers to talk to each other became a giant multi-billion-dollar startup.

6. Revenue model pivot

Sometimes the product is fantastic and people love it, but you're not making any money, or the customers aren't willing to pay enough to make it worthwhile. You can experiment with different business models and settle on the one which makes sense. Let's say you are extremely valuable to a few power users, you can shift to a usage-based model to monetise them while encouraging new users who get a cheap introductory price.

7. Total pivot

The most extreme pivot where you're almost an entirely new company. This is where nothing seems to be working. You've got a great team, but no results. Twitter famously did an internal hackathon after realising Odeo, the original podcast platform, wasn't gaining traction. Total pivots become more viable when you've got external capital and supportive investors. If existing investors don't believe in the new product direction, you can return their money or have another investor buy them out to avoid potential issues.

You may need to shut down and set up a clean company if a critical section of the current stakeholders isn't behind you. This provides the founders with a fresh cap table and eliminates any ambiguity.

Pulling off a pivot

There are a couple of important factors that I want you to consider when you're going through a pivot.

Align your stakeholders

You can't have unhappy passengers if you want your pivot to work.

- **Cofounders** - The relative value-add and passion of each founder may not be the same post-pivot. Is it best for the founding team to split up so the pivot has the best chance?

- **Team** - Do you have the right team for the new plan? Give them the option to leave if they don't want to be a part of the new mission. There's no point in keeping top talent who don't want to be there.

- **Investors** - Early stage investors should expect pivots, but you might not fit some of their theses anymore. If these investors have a significant portion of your capital, it may be better to return what you can and shut down, then restart. They won't invest in further rounds and complicate the cap table.

- **Other stakeholders** - Do any of your partners/clients have dependencies on you? Can you smooth the transition so they have a reasonable adjustment period?

Commit

Be decisive. Don't kinda be the old startup and kinda be the new one. You'll confuse everyone and be mediocre everywhere. Eliminate parts of the business if they don't align with the new direction. Go back to first principles. Reassess everything from your team to your customer validation to your distribution channels. If you're going to pivot, do it properly and don't wait too long to pull the trigger, as the motivation of those around you can only decrease.

Summary

- Set a long-term vision known as a Big Hairy Audacious Goal or a North Star that keeps you focused on why you're working so hard.

- Set short-term targets using the OKR model to stay on track and keep accountable.

- Revenue is usually the best primary target, with retention and CAC as good secondary metrics.

- Prevent overwhelm by avoiding shiny lights, and use if-then plans, not-to-do lists and done lists.

- Pivots are fundamental changes to your startup which are more significant than regular iterations.

- Burnout, headturning, customers not caring, team struggles, investor not biting and stagnation are signals to pivot.

- You can pivot customer segment, problem, product, feature-as-a-product, internal to external, revenue model and/or a total pivot.

- Pull off your pivot by aligning stakeholders and not half-assing it.

Exercises

- Set your Big Hairy Audacious Goal.

- Set realistic short-term goals based on your resources and other startups.

- Figure out what would force you to pivot and keep track of these signals.

Chapter 7
Planning on one page

Traditional business advisors will teach entrepreneurs to make a robust business plan. You'd write down all the little details in a thick document. You'd have specific numbers based on assumptions with a high degree of confidence. You can use similar businesses to benchmark, and there are fewer unknown unknowns. Startups aren't the same beast. You're likely building something no one has done before. You're going to need to iterate and pivot repeatedly before you get it right. Most of your assumptions will be wrong. Investing your precious time in making a proper document would be a waste of time.

Yet you do want to track your experiments and gain clarity on exactly what you're building. You can do this on just one page. There are many tools to do this, such as the Business Model Canvas by Alexander Osterwalder and Yves Pigneur, and the Lean Canvas by Ash Maurya. I'll share my One Page Startup script in this chapter. Don't create a plan to tick a box. The exercise has a purpose. The goal is to have the key elements laid out so you (and others) can dissect and iterate.

> *"If I had more time, I would have written a shorter letter."*
>
> Blaise Pascal

You'll find the plan isn't easier to write because it's only one page. You might struggle in your first few attempts to find the correct wording. This pain is good. It's progress. The trick is crafting the plan throughout your day. When you're thinking in the shower. When you're daydreaming in a meeting. When you talk to a customer and have a light bulb moment.

The One Page Startup script is just a representation of what's happening in your brain. If you're like me, your brain can be chaotic, and you'll value something structured!

One Page Startup script

We're solving: [Problem]

For: [Customer segment]

Because: [Pain]

They've tried: [Best alternative]

We're building: [Solution]

Which is better because: [10x Feature]

Our potential is: [Market size]

We're best to build because: [Team]

We're going to monetise through: [Business model]

We're going to gain customers by: [Distribution channels]

Our vision is: [BHAG]

We're going to measure success along the way by: [Key metrics]

Our major costs will be: [Costs]

It's that simple. You can now see the significant elements of what you're building in one place. Put only the most compelling answer in each section. Once you start getting into X and Y and Z, you're losing focus.

You can use this as a script when explaining your startup to others by cutting off the costs at the end. You can modify this as a script when pitching to investors by changing the last line to, "We're raising money to pay for". Here's some extra guidance if you're stuck on any section:

We're solving: [Problem]

Avoid the temptation to list every grievance from your customer research in Chapter 2. Use language anyone can understand.

For: [Customer segment]

Picking anyone who suffers from the problem is not specific enough. Use psychographic and demographic details to establish one well-defined group. If you have multiple customer segments, such as in a marketplace, then create a plan for each one. You can also create plans for your ECP and your ICP, which you defined in Chapter 2.

Because: [Pain]

Squeeze the pain with what makes it so urgent and hair on fire. What are the consequences of your solution not existing? Customers should have made this clear in Chapter 2.

They've tried: [Best alternative]

From customer research in Chapter 2, you should know what your customer base has tried before which hasn't solved their pain.

We're building: [Solution]

Your iterations through Chapter 3 and beyond mean you can say what you're creating without any fluff or jargon.

Which is better because: [10x Feature]

You learned in Chapter 4 how to showcase your unique value proposition, where you become the only real solution, not one of many.

Our potential is: [Market size]

You researched this back in Chapter 2, and should know both how big the initial market is and where it can scale if you capture your ICP.

We're best to build because: [Team]

You know what makes a good founding team from Chapter 1, now put each cofounder's highlights.

We're going to monetise through: [Business model]

Chapter 5 talked through your business model options. You can put price hypotheses here and update if you're incorrect.

We're going to gain customers by: [Distribution channels]

Chapter 5 was all about earning attention. Until you know what works, you can put your best guess here.

Our vision is: [BHAG]

This should excite you and inspire others, as you saw in Chapter 6.

We're going to measure success along the way by: [Key metrics]

Chapter 6 also grounded you in what your immediate focus should be and how you'll track your progress.

Our major costs will be: [Costs]

The least fun bit, but Chapter 5 covered in detail all the costs, so you should know what you'll need to spend to survive and scale.

Summary

- The One Page Startup script brings everything you've learned in this book in one place.

- Use it as an exercise as often as you need to help bring clarity to the chaos.

Exercises

- Do the plan! It takes no time at all.

- If you don't have a startup yet, you can run through the plan for other people's startups - this is a great way to understand what and why people are doing it.

Chapter 8
Networking

I hate how outsiders are overlooked because they don't have the right connections. You can do everything else right, but who you know matters. The ecosystem likes to portray itself as meritocratic, but if you went to an expensive school and your mates' dads are all venture capitalists, then you're going to get funding faster. Networking can bring investors, customers, partners and simply friends who understand your struggles.

You'll feel icky when it's done transactionally, but it's not realistic to be best friends with everyone you want to connect to. You've got to find a happy middle ground, and it's an art form rather than a science. I went from being a nobody in the UK startup world to leading one of the country's largest founder and investor communities in less than three years. I know hundreds of investors and thousands of venture-backed founders. I'm sharing my RSVP formula, which fueled my journey:

- Resourceful

- Specific

- Visible

- Powerful

Being resourceful is table stakes to shift your conversations into the mutually interesting zone. Being specific, visible and powerful stack on top of each other.

E.g. If you are incredibly visible, you might get away with being less of the others, but it will benefit you to be strong in all.

Resourceful

Being self-sufficient is a secret hack. Networking is most effective when you focus on building human connections, not fact-finding.

You're told at school and work that there's no such thing as a stupid question. But teachers and managers are paid to help you. It's not the job of other founders and investors to personally teach you things you could find out yourself. The situation is different in a workshop or Q&A session, of course, but other interactions don't revolve around you. You want to be as informed as possible before using up someone else's time. People like to help people who help themselves. The last thing you want is to come across like a parasite in networking interactions. Avoid asking people to answer:

- **Generic questions** - What is X? How do I Y? You should never build relationships by asking questions which a search engine or an AI tool can give a reasonable answer to. I'm shocked at how many people choose to DM me like I'm their personal encyclopaedia.

- **Public detail questions** - What's your story? What does your company do? These are lazy questions. Go to their profile. Go to their company's website. Listen to podcasts. These are great questions if you're meeting someone unexpected for the first time, but not if you're reaching out.

Many of my role models don't know I exist. You can reverse engineer most achievements people have made with a little effort. Use the advice they've shared in public to enjoy their insights without asking to "pick their brains". If I can do one public service through this book, please never use that phrase. Don't tell someone you're a huge fan, but then appear not to know basic information about them. You'll find your mentors are more engaged if you're not asking them the basic stuff they've already repeated a million times.

You can be intelligent about networking by going to where the doors are already open. You don't need to mass spam people for knowledge or connections. Bae HQ offers online resources and hosts events and programmes for founders. We're one organisation of many in this space (though we're my favourite!). I also co-lead Pitch and Run in London, where you can meet people from the startup ecosystem every week and get fit at the same time. There are all kinds of opportunities to meet people. You could find options in your space easily if you take 5 minutes to search. Follow the groups which appeal to you and sign up when they post something relevant.

While no one person will be your saviour, if there's someone you dream about meeting, you probably can by paying attention to their event schedule. You earn brownie points by meeting people in a way which is convenient for them rather than expecting them to bend for you.

Specific

You have to say who you are, what you want and why the other person should care when asking for other people's time. Once they've spent time on you, they'll never get it back until there's a giant leap in quantum physics. Likewise, you won't get your time back either. Being specific in your requests allows you to get a quick rejection if someone isn't a good fit for you. You can redirect your attention elsewhere.

The opportunity cost of your time increases as you become more successful. Let's say you believe your time is worth £10 an hour. Your benchmark for accepting random requests is whether you think the outcome will be worth more. I attended coffee meetings with dubious potential returns at the start of Bae HQ because I had to experiment. As you scale, let's say your time is now worth £100 an hour. You must start rejecting requests you once accepted. High-value people prioritise ruthlessly. They have more demands for their attention than hours in the day. They need to lower the priority of something else on their list to carve out space for you. I don't take any one-to-one meetings outside of programmes anymore unless it's paid or with a large potential sponsor. Consider this simple rule:

> The more valuable your current use of time, the higher the bar to accept new demands.

You need to convince the other person that you meet their bar for them to be willing to spend time with you. You'll get ignored or fobbed off if you don't give your target enough information to decide how to prioritise you. Ambiguity is the enemy of networking. Don't force a busy person to guess why you want to talk to them. When you drop a vague request to them, you're disrespecting the value of their time.

When you meet someone in person, you have more time to build trust and set up a follow-up meeting. When messaging online, you need to be much more efficient. These messages all suck:

- Hi.

- Call me.

- How are you?

- Can I pick your brain?

- We need to grab a coffee.

- Let's hop on a quick call.

- People said we should talk.

- I want to tell you what I'm up to.

- I need to talk to you about something.

- I've got a potential opportunity for you.

- I've got something which will be interesting to you.

How can the person possibly tell if you're worth their time from these messages? You can do better! You might still get ignored or rejected. But you want the other person to make an informed decision rather than a default no. Answer these questions in your outreach:

Who exactly are you?

This is a single line in a message which says your role at your startup and what it does without jargon. They should be able to tell whether you're relevant and credible. You can add storytelling in person to make yourself more memorable. Gauge the other person and tailor the parts of your background which will be most interesting to them.

What exactly do you want?

Ask in a way which gets a quick rejection if you're talking to someone who isn't interested. There's no point in being fluffy, convincing the person to meet you and then being disappointed after you wasted your time on a coffee across town. E.g., if you want investment and the person doesn't invest in your industry. Make sure the person understands the time, money and energy costs of your ask.

Why exactly should they care?

You're not entitled to anyone else's time. You're building a startup for your mission, and you're trying to grow. The other person has their own priorities. How are you helping them? What credibility do you have?

Visible

You learned about how to earn attention in Chapter 4. When people already recognise you or know about your startup, they're more likely to give you their time. The trust and familiarity can lower their guard. Here are some tactics:

Original content

The easiest way to do this at scale is through content, as many people will know who you are at once. Be prepared for parasocial relationships if you go down this route. It's uncomfortable for people to know who you are, and you don't know anything about them, in my experience. Yet you can leverage this into a significant advantage. Let's say we met each other once, and we added each other on social media. I post daily, and you never post. You listen to my podcasts and read this book (thanks!). When we meet 6 months later, you will know everything I've been up to and have seen my face dozens of times. What will I know?

Founders underestimate the positive compounding effect of consistent visibility. Everyone who consumes my content (and likes me!) is someone who can recommend me for opportunities. People have opened doors for me, which I didn't even know existed. To make a lasting impression on someone through one short interaction is almost impossible. Content can top it up.

The social-proof effect also helps even without direct contact. I only have tens of thousands of followers across platforms at the time of writing, but this puts me in the top 1%. If you can get to the same level, then others will assume you must be worth speaking to. Otherwise, why do so many people follow you?

Orbit

When you have a high-value target connection, you should try to reach out, but be aware that you may get lost in their heap of requests. You can gain an edge if you've orbited around them beforehand. Few people do the underrated tactic of engaging with their target's public social media posts. Most people don't have the confidence to do this. If you're commenting on their posts every day and adding value, they're going to notice you. You're actually helping them by boosting their visibility, which they'll be grateful for. When they host a virtual event, turn up and ask an insightful question. When they're speaking at an event in person, turn up and introduce yourself.

When you eventually have a specific ask for them, they're going to know who you are and be more likely to prioritise you.

Swarm

The most valuable people in the ecosystem are difficult to reach. A team manages their inbound, and they rarely turn up to public events. They rush off after speaking at conferences. You've got to swallow your ego and make smart moves. These people rely on an inner circle of people they trust to filter their connections. You want to nurture trust with this group. Don't target the other hyperbusy people in the group! So many people ask me to connect them to my podcast guests without considering how much I have on my plate myself.

Your best bet is the junior employees on their team and their friends who are less in demand. Don't request a warm introduction to begin with. Be authentic because these connections are valuable in themselves. Treat them like humans, it's not that hard! When someone keeps hearing your name from people they trust, they rate you by proxy. If the first warm intro doesn't work, surely the tenth will.

Powerful

Let's get an ugly truth out of the way. The more power and influence you have, the more everyone will want to talk to you. You can wish the world weren't this way, but it is. You can have zero visibility. Remember, we said in Chapter 4 that we can't name most billionaires. Yet if one of them wanted to have coffee, I'd say yes immediately, and you would too. These people have high power with low visibility, and the rules of networking are different for them. You'd be clever to target these people when you outreach. They're likely to get fewer requests than others because of their lack of public persona.

But I'm guessing you're not a billionaire. For the rest of us, how can we use being powerful to help us in networking? The trick is not to think of power in a linear sense. Wealth has an obvious way to measure success, but you can lean into your differences to stand out. You could be an insider to a world which other people want insight into. I've recorded 400+ podcasts, which few people have done, but people far more financially powerful would love to replicate. Other people will want to talk to me after releasing this book. You could be someone's target audience and have a community of others whom they want to target. We've worked with organisations much larger than us because they want what we have.

Vulnerability can be another great leveller. If you're able to put into words what others feel but can't express, they'll want to hang out with you. While this isn't a good conversation initiator, it can be an effective way to create a deeper, more human bond. You stop trying to pretend and just be.

Summary

- Use the RSVP formula to build meaningful relationships with people you admire.

- Being resourceful allows you to skip the boring questions people are sick of and focus on a human connection instead.

- Being specific allows others to gauge whether spending time with you is a good use of their limited hours in the day - answer who, what, and why.

- Being visible allows you to get access where you might not otherwise because people have trust in you from your content or because you've orbited or swarmed them.

- Being powerful allows you to have others want to talk to you because they believe they can learn from you.

Exercises

- Keep track of all educational questions you want answered and use search engines or AI for answers.

- Pause before messaging anyone to reflect on whether you could find the answer yourself instead.

- Craft a one-liner which oozes credibility so others can quickly assess you.

- Practice being concise and specific in your requests.

- Decide whether you want to take the content route to gain recognition in your industry.

- Build out a list of high-value targets and work out how you can orbit or swarm around them.

- Write down all the different ways you can add value, which could attract others.

Chapter 9
Hiring early employees

Your first full-time hires will set the culture for everyone who comes after them. And to be blunt, A players don't want to work for B players. Your ability to attract top-quality talent is critical for scaling. As we discussed in Chapter 5, you shouldn't hire until you need to and your finances can sustain paying wages.

You are the example

Hiring is awkward if you haven't done it before. I didn't like the power dynamic when interviewing for our first employee. You know what giving a job offer means to everyone who applies, and rejecting them is tough. But you're the founder, and it's your responsibility.

All cofounders should be on board for at least the first few hires. It's that important. You'll usually have one founder involved, even at the scaleup stage. Hiring is one of the last tasks you delegate to other members of the team. A bad team choice can completely tank your startup's performance. The right one can send you to the moon.

You should be interviewing candidates yourself and show clear engagement. They're joining a company where you have an extraordinary say. You've wasted your time and theirs if you can't work together. If you want extra validation, you can ask a friend who is more experienced with hiring to interview the candidate in addition.

The ping pong tables and random quirky perks of yesteryear are less in fashion now. Don't insult candidates' intelligence by thinking you can sway them like this. They're judging:

- Will they feel valued?

- Will you inspire them?

- Will they fit in with the team?

- Will they be on a rocket ship?

- Will this be a smart move for their career?

- Will they truly work on something meaningful?

Remember, candidates will have access to every piece of public information about you and your startup. Funding announcements are often better at attracting key hires than customers. Top candidates will rule themselves out if they don't like what they read about you online.

Who to hire

Let's kill the worst mistake you can make now. Don't hire someone you meet who sweet-talks you into hiring them when there's no business need. I've met pushy characters who insist they want to help me, but for a fee which is unjustifiable. You can split roles into two groups:

- **Value creator** - Is your business stagnating because of a lack of resources, but could be generating more revenue? Will 2+2=5? You want to hire people who will increase revenue per employee.

- **Value protector** - What are the greatest risks in your business? Can hiring someone in-house mean your startup is much more likely to survive? You can generally hire service providers rather than take the function in-house unless you're in a regulated industry. Put off hiring value protectors until there's value worth protecting!

Generalists, such as founders' associates, operations managers and Chief of Operations, may do tasks in both groups. Many startups I know hire generalists first who can act as extensions of the founders and roll up their sleeves to put out any fire. Specialists work best when you have a clear scope for exactly where they'll be needed. Always judge based on your situation, not what you've seen others do.

Where to find them

People you've worked with before

The simplest path. You have a known entity, and you know them far more deeply than any interview process can reveal. You'll be certain there's chemistry, and you'll have seen first-hand their abilities.

Referrals from your network

Here's where there's some controversy. Many founders swear by hiring through recommendations. These referrals reduce some of the risk of the unknown. Yet this obviously limits opportunities for talented people who don't have a network. Of course, the only referrals that matter come from those whom you think are competent themselves.

Competitors

Controversial again, but you'd be naive to think it's not happening. Look at companies you respect in your niche and add employees. Let them see your journey, and when it comes time to hire, you can send them the job to see if they're interested.

Fans

The next person I hire will have read this book. They'll have listened to my podcast and signed up to my newsletter. People who use your product are some of the best to hire because they relate to the problem you're trying to solve. They will come in with a strong sense of what your brand stands for.

Recruiters

There's a heavy cost associated with using recruiters. It might not be the best first port of call unless you're struggling to fill a space. Yet spending a few thousand on fees for someone who you hope will help you make millions can be a reasonable trade-off for senior roles.

Open applications

The fairest way of all. You may find incredible candidates who would have never applied otherwise, and just be aware that AI has led to an increase in low-effort applications. Whichever methods you use above, it's also good to have open applications, as the more you see, the more precise your idea of what good looks like.

What to look for

I'm not going to dive into the series of options you have for assessing candidates before hiring them. There's a mix of best practices and personal preferences. You should be aware that the best candidates have options, and if you string them along, they'll go elsewhere. Don't try to innovate when it comes to contracts. Keep it simple and make sure you're following the laws of your country! However you choose to run your process, these traits are key:

Competency

You're hiring for a role which needs to be done, and you need to trust the person you hire can do it effectively. Don't hire a developer who can't ship!

Potential questions:

- Ask them to explain the process they'd take for solving a problem.

- Give an example of a task they'd be expected to handle and ask them what they'd do.

- Do a practical test where possible.

A personal pet peeve - don't ask candidates to do anything which should be paid consulting work during the interview process. Your goal is to learn about the candidate, not get work done for free.

Startup readiness

Working at a startup is significantly different to working at a larger company, and you'll want to test if the employee knows what they're getting into. They won't have the same predictable career ladder or stability they'd get elsewhere. They'll be an extension of the founder to later employees. When their job role shifts, will they adapt or sulk? Interest in lower salary for employee stock options is a green flag that they're looking to stick around for the long term.

Potential questions:

- Why do you want to work for a startup?
- Are you also applying to large companies? Why?
- What's the hardest thing you've ever done?
- When have you worked in a small team effectively?

Mission orientation

You can't pay them what they'd earn at a larger company. They've got to be there because they care. You want them to be as obsessed with the problem as you are.

Potential questions:

- What motivates you to do your best work?
- Why do you care about what we're trying to do?
- What are you sacrificing to work with us compared to your other options?

Cost effectiveness

Hiring someone because they're cheap can and will backfire. You pay in other ways with issues you'll need to deal with. When hiring junior employees, you need to account for the time you'll spend training and checking their work. Sometimes a senior employee who hits the ground running is worth the extra cost.

Potential questions:

- What support would you expect from us?

- When have you taken ownership of a project?

- How do you like to be managed?

Blindspot coverage

DEI goes through seasons of being in and out of fashion, but diversity of thought isn't a nice-to-have. The team is above the individual. You need to look at the extra perspectives and skills a potential hire brings. Can they bring insight you're missing to increase the value of your offering?

Potential questions:

- You've researched us before this interview. What do you think we could do differently?

- What potential opportunities do you think we're currently missing out on / should consider?

- What concerns came up for you when researching us?

Working style

Startup founders are split between diehard remote-working disciples and others who swear the only way to work is in person. Some founders demand long hours from employees, whereas others are more flexible. Some founders communicate bluntly, whereas others prefer structured, thoughtful meetings. Your founding team has preferences across these areas, and hiring someone who doesn't enjoy working in the same style as you is doomed to fail. It's crucial you explain expectations during the hiring process so candidates can count themselves out if they're not a fan of how you run things.

Potential questions:

- How would you describe your communication style?

- How do you deal with conflict?

- When have you worked the hardest?

Retaining the best people

Let's say you manage to land your perfect employee. They've settled in well, and they start accelerating your revenue. You now need to make sure you don't lose them.

Onboarding

A new hire needs proper onboarding to have the best chance of succeeding at your startup. They can't read your mind, so don't expect them to! No employee will ever work out for you if you're not willing to set them up with:

- Clearly defined roles and responsibility outlines, which can be adjusted when needed.

- Expectations of the standards they're expected to hit.

- The necessary tools, resources and contacts to do their job effectively.

Probation periods are standard for new employees. They provide both you and the new team member a low-risk way to assess whether you're well-suited for each other.

Performance analysis

Team members will have a decent sense of how well they're doing. You should work with them so they have a measurable track record. But they don't know how well you think they're doing unless they say, and ultimately, you're in charge of their future opportunities. Give regular feedback so they should never be surprised if they are let go:

- Appreciation when they shine.

- Pointers on when they could do better.

- Consequences when they do wrong.

Not every employee will work out. You must let them go once you've shared negative feedback and they haven't shown improvement despite reasonable support. Yet you must act fast when it's a behaviour issue. You're a team, not a family. This goes two ways, though, and you should be receptive to feedback from your team. You have to have the structure in place for them to thrive.

Roadmap

Take the time to understand what motivates the team member and where they want to go. Understand whether their current role is meeting their expectations and where it's more or less fulfilling. Your startup's resource demands will change, and this means there's always an opportunity for them. You can map out your future needs and where they could step up. Don't forget you have to put the business above the individual, and you can't promote someone who hasn't proven they can handle it.

There may come a time when the relationship ends without any need for ill will. Perhaps the company has pivoted so dramatically that they're no longer a fit. Maybe they've changed their dreams and ambitions and think they'll be better served elsewhere. Regardless of the situation, try to end on the best terms you can. You never know when your paths may cross again. If they become a founder, you might even become each other's customers!

Summary

- Cofounders are the examples and the magnets for early hires.

- You should be heavily involved in the process and reflect on the quality you want to bring in.

- Hire based on a provable business need rather than what others tell you to do.

- Use a variety of methods to get the job out there and get the best candidate pool.

- Hire for competency, startup readiness, mission orientation, cost effectiveness, blindspot coverage and working style.

- Retain the best talent by maintaining transparency with them and helping set out a roadmap of where they could progress.

Exercises

- Assess what comes up when people search you and your startup - is it up to date and accurate? Does it reflect what you want a candidate to see?

- Keep track of gaps where you'd want to hire in the future and the intensity of the need.

- Maintain a strong network of capable people who could be part of your candidate pool someday.

- Track what matters to you in terms of working style, mission orientation and blindspot coverage.

Chapter 10
Funding from external sources

You're going to hate me for saying this. I put this chapter near the end of the book on purpose. Because many founders don't need external funding as early as they think they do. Be obsessed with problems and customers rather than fundraising. Nailing the earlier chapters means you'll have a strong business case for whatever route you choose.

Certain types of companies need significant funding upfront to develop their products. Most startups don't. But they can use the external funding to scale faster and reach their potential. The impact on stress levels can be immense - especially for those with weaker pre-existing personal finances.

Yet, as we explore funding options, remember money isn't the solution to all problems. Having too much money can make you lazy. You don't optimise enough and get overconfident. You'll hire people you don't need and overcomplicate the business. Are you using your resources as efficiently as you can? Do you know how you'll spend the extra cash in an effective way?

Types of funding

Payback-free

Where you can receive funding without financial payback.

- Grants
- R&D tax credits
- Competition & prizes
- Non-equity crowdfunding

Debt

Where a financial institution allows you to borrow.

- Startup-specific loans
- Revenue-based financing
- Venture debt

Equity

Where investors take a share in your company.

- Friends and family

- Equity crowdfunding

- Angel

- Angel syndicates

- Startup accelerators and incubators

- Venture capital

- Corporate Venture Capital

Payback-free

Grants

The closest to a free lunch you get as a founder. You get capital without needing to give away any equity in your company or needing to pay the money back. If you can take grant money, then do! The catch is that grants can be difficult to win:

1. The ecosystem is complex, and knowing about grants you're eligible for isn't always straightforward.

2. The process can involve a considerable amount of paperwork with little guidance. There are people (expensive people) who have full-time careers writing grant applications for founders. Even with this, you could fail and not get any feedback on why.

3. There can be strict boundaries on what the money can be used for, which may fit awkwardly into your plans. This could prevent you from prioritising the most critical areas from a business perspective at your startup.

4. Some grants will have conditions that require you to return the funding at a later date. Always read the fine print!

Companies that are making a social impact or doing genuine research are best positioned to win grant funding. The government is the biggest provider of grants through various bodies. You can also get grants from social impact foundations. They can have a particular mandate for socioeconomic issues or underrepresented entrepreneurs.

R&D tax credits/relief

The slightly awkward cousin of grants, but still free money! You could be eligible depending on what you're building and where your startup is based. The rules change too often for my liking, but when the stars align, they enable you to get more done for less. Be aware that you generally have to claim the money back rather than receiving it up front. A specialist can help if you think you could be eligible.

Competitions and prizes

Pitch days with financial prizes can be a slick way of earning funding in the early days while practising your pitching. You'd be surprised how many pitch days there are in major cities. The cash can add up over time, even if each prize is only a few thousand. You can leverage hackathons with prizes in the same way.

As a long-term strategy, it doesn't work just because there are only a few competitions with meaningful prizes like SaaStock. It can be an alternative or complement to writing grant applications. You never know who is in the audience and how they could help your business scale.

Non-equity crowdfunding

Platforms exist which allow startups to raise capital for projects without needing to give away shares or pay back the backers! If your product is mission-driven, people could be willing to support it because they care. The rewards can range from discounts to customised products or appreciation.

Debt

Startups are too risky for most traditional business banks. It's understandable. They lose money when you fail! They want a lengthy financial history as well as a transparent, predictable cash flow. Something you won't have at the start. You might get lucky if you had traditional businesses in the past and have a reputation with a local bank.

The better the end result of your startup, the cheaper debt is relative to equity. Loans have a predictable range of total cost, whereas equity is far more uncertain:

- Borrowing £100k
    - Predictable interest repayments costing tens of thousands and potentially hundreds, depending on your terms.
    - You may still have to pay back if the startup fails if you gave a personal guarantee.
- Taking an investment of £100k
    - The "cost" is in the share of the upside of growth you give up. If you gave 1% of your company away for £100k and you become a billion-dollar startup, that stake is now worth £10m!
    - Yet if you go bust, then the stake is worthless and you haven't given up anything.

Here are some debt options:

Startup-specific loans

Some banks and fintechs have products designed for startups - they generally have higher interest rates. Yet governments want to encourage innovation and back programmes depending on where you live. These loans can also come with free mentorship and support. You'll need to create a business plan and a cash flow forecast to access the money. While these may feel like a chore, they help you to focus your thoughts, much like grant applications do.

The UK government funds The Startup Loans Company, which lets founders borrow up to £25k. It's per founder, so you could borrow £100k if you have four cofounders. The interest rate is 6%, and you have 1-5 years to repay it as of 2025. The scheme has funded over 100k entrepreneurs so far.

Revenue-based financing

This is an innovative way to fund your startup where you take a loan, but your repayments are based on a % of your revenue rather than fixed amounts. You have less stress in weaker months, and you pay more in stronger months. This flexibility is excellent for many startups, and approval can be fast.

The challenge for startups is that you can only get revenue-based financing if you actually have revenue! The total interest can be more than regular loans, which is a price you pay for the flexibility. This model works for SaaS and e-commerce startups and others with subscription-based revenue.

Quick maths: You have £1m revenue per month. You take out a loan of £100k. You have a 5% fee. If you stick to the average, you repay in 2 months. If your revenue drops to £500k, then you repay in 4 months.

Venture debt

While the name can mislead some, venture debt is a loan, not an investment. It's only accessible to those who've raised venture capital in most cases as a proxy of trustworthiness. The interest is higher than traditional loans (have you spotted a trend?). It's a useful way to extend the runway between rounds, but read the terms carefully. You can be forced to repay early if overly ambitious targets called covenants are not met.

Equity

When you raise funding through equity, you're trading money today for upside in the potential value of the company in the future with investors. Don't confuse this with revenue.

The way this worked wasn't clear to me until I became an angel investor. Simplified - founders create new shares in the startup rather than giving existing shares. The ledger of who owns what % of your startup is listed on the cap table. If you want to raise £1m, you create as many shares as needed for the slice of the company to meet investor needs. You don't want to be giving up more than 10-15% round as a rule of thumb. Let's say you raise at a £5m pre-money valuation, this means the value of the existing shares is £5m. Once you have the investment, the post-money valuation is £6m. You and your investors have to wait for an exit event to make any profit on your shares. There's more about that in Chapter 12.

For now, you need to understand the different types of equity funding rounds. They're used inconsistently, but give you an idea of where you are:

- **Friends and family** = the first investors at the start of the journey.

- **Pre-seed** = Investors who invest before any real traction - this is usually angel money with potentially family office or VC.

- **Seed** = Traction has started to take off, but product market fit is not quite solidified. This is where most VCs begin to get interested.

- **Series A** = Rounds start to get bigger and more dominated by VCs. Series A is where product market fit is more or less proven, and it's now time to really scale.

- **Series B+** = More and more money for international expansion and further products.

Some governments offer incentives to encourage individual investors to back early-stage startups. The UK provides SEIS and EIS, at the time of writing, where you can apply for a special status which allows your investors to claim back income tax. The schemes can change depending on government policy, but be sure to check out options before fundraising. Let's dive into all the different types of investors across the rounds:

Family and friends

Many founders turn to those who know them well first before reaching out more widely. Your friends and family have way more due diligence on you as a person, and can have more confidence in you compared to anyone you meet fresh. You might have the opposite effect on people, of course. Social mobility is a significant challenge in the startup space because this source of funding relies on rich friends and family!

You have to be smart about your relationships. Your friends and family must know the risks and should understand they could lose all their money. There are many cases of relationships turning bitter where someone invests and feels like they were misled by the founders. How would you feel if you invest in a friend who parties every weekend and their startup ends up going bust?

The fear of letting down those close to them is motivation for some founders and gives them extra fire in their bellies. Friends and family rounds are often informal, which makes the process faster but can lead to headaches down the line. Make sure there are contracts where you can, because you never know how friendships will break down when there's money involved.

Equity crowdfunding

Using online platforms, you can open your cap table up to many smaller investors. In theory, if you don't have rich friends and family, this gives you access to a broad range of non-institutional investors. It can be especially useful when you have a large social media following or you have a strong, loyal customer base.

You need to tell a powerful story which has viral potential to succeed. A crowdfunding campaign can be fantastic for marketing efforts. Many new people hear about your startup, and there's potential for press coverage and organic sharing. The practical side is a little more complex. Most crowdfunding platforms require you to have already raised a significant proportion of what you want to raise. So if you don't have a strong immediate base, you'll struggle. This is for optics. They want to be able to say you're X% funded on day one. They don't want to list startups which are unlikely to raise the money.

You can damage morale by being unprepared and failing to raise funds through crowdfunding. The regulatory compliance and platform fees are no joke too. Do the analysis carefully before crowdfunding. Be sure you have the gravitas to attract the investment you need, and forecast the sales uplift through the marketing efforts. You may find it cheaper and less stressful to raise from angels or angel networks.

Angel investors

Angel investors can be the most confusing of all the different types of funding. They are individuals who invest their personal capital into startups. There are several qualifications to be able to invest in startups legally, based on where you live. But the two main buckets of qualified angel investors are:

- High-Net-Worth Individuals who meet financial criteria.

- Sophisticated investors who have proven they understand the risks of investing in private markets.

The truth is, angel investors can have almost nothing in common with each other in how they operate and how they invest. Some are super angels who invest in dozens of companies, some even 100+. They've generated massive personal wealth through their own startup exits or successful careers. Others rarely invest and take a lot of convincing to part with their money. Some invest £100k+ into a single company, while others write much smaller 4-figure checks. I fall into the second group with my six angel investments ranging between £1k and £5k. Some angel investors are purely financially motivated, and others want to back impact in specific industries or groups of people.

The best angel investors bring significant value with their expertise and connections. My visibility brings attention to my portfolio companies, and those who might invest or work with them will see my connection in a positive way (I hope). The variation amongst angel investors means greater optionality too. Some will move very fast. Others will move painfully slowly and waste your time.

Angel syndicates

Angel syndicates are just groups of angel investors who invest together. This allows them to write smaller checks and have the safety of numbers. If their friends are also investing, then they must be making the right decision, right?

For founders, angel syndicates are great to simplify the cap table and reduce the pain of talking to each investor individually. The syndicate leads may do some form of due diligence on behalf of the group and put the questions into a structured format.

A well-regarded syndicate backing you can be a positive signal to later investors. The investor world is smaller than you think, and if angels in the syndicate have a strong reputation, they can give referrals. You might find that even if the overall syndicate doesn't invest, you'll be put on the radar of individual investors who will.

Startup accelerators and incubators

There's no consensus definition of what exactly an accelerator and what exactly an incubator are. Each individual programme has its own set of rules, which can be the opposite of another. And not all programmes actually financially invest. Zoom out. Both are about giving you access to resources you couldn't easily get otherwise, such as expert mentorship and access to networks. The best programmes are highly competitive and are intense in their demands on you.

An incubator is a programme for the earliest-stage companies in the idea phase. They can be long programmes, which are months or even years or shorter sprints. Our IncuBaetor programme is the latter, and we don't offer any financing. Others do.

An accelerator is a programme which usually ends with a company raising their first major round, but this isn't a rule. Accelerators are more likely to take equity, but this isn't always a rule either. It's to speed up a startup which already has something going for it. Y Combinator is the most famous accelerator, and they offer all startups the same terms.

A good accelerator can fast-track your startup like almost nothing else. A bad accelerator can be a total waste of your time. Check with programme alumni before giving away equity to a programme.

Family offices

Like angel investors, family offices can have wildly different theses and ways of working. They are bodies set up to manage the wealth of High-Net-Worth Individuals and Ultra-High-Net-Worth Individuals or groups of them. The most prominent family offices can write large checks to rival venture capital. They can be much more flexible with their terms compared to VCs because they're investing their own family's resources.

Family offices can be the hardest investors to reach, because many don't want to be public, and instead rely on warm introductions from those they trust. Like angels, some will be financially motivated only, whereas others will want to invest in companies that have missions they believe in. Family offices can be some of the best value-add investors, especially when they're exited founders themselves.

Venture capital

The one you've all been waiting for. Venture capital is the big dog in the funding scene for startups, even if the assets under management are small compared to private equity, hedge funds and other institutions. The venture capital model is boom or bust, where they are looking for companies which can 100x and IPO. They want the Netflixs, Ubers and Airbnbs of this world. Can you get to £100M annual revenue in the next 10 years? This roughly translates to unicorn (billion-dollar valuation) status. Venture capital is wrong for most businesses which aren't even trying to get to that level.

Let's explain quickly how the VC model works. Venture capitalists are investing other people's money. Limited Partners (LPs) invest in VC funds with the goal of dramatically beating market returns. LPs can be pension funds, governments and HNWIs. I'm a micro LP in two funds, but I'm an anomaly and way poorer than the average LP because of my access to the network through Bae HQ.

VCs will have what's called a thesis, which is their way of differentiating from other funds. This could mean they are specialised in investing in a particular geography, industry or founder demographics. VCs often charge 2% of the assets under management per year and take 20% of the returns generated by the fund. This means over the typical 10-year life cycle of a fund, the fund targets a return of at least 3x, which is harder than it sounds due to dilution.

When you consider that most startups will fail to deliver any return to the fund, they need the big wins to make the fund math work. It's not worth a venture capitalist investing in a small play. They want high risk and higher reward. Most will want some level of traction to prove you've got the ability to deliver this. At the early stages, they'll be analysing you to incredible depth to see if they think you're the type of founder who could build a billion-dollar company.

They'll take a significant chunk of your equity and sign terms which favour them. Yet if you really want to build a world-changing company, the right VC can open up all the doors to make it possible. Many VCs are now competing with each other on the hottest deals, and spend a lot of time thinking about how to be the highest value add to their founders.

Corporate Venture Capital (CVC)

CVCs are arms of large corporations that invest in companies which align with their strategic interests. They've got very different structures, which makes it hard to generalise. For instance, a bank might invest in fintech companies so they can become early adopters and gain an edge over competitors. A large energy company might invest in emerging renewable energy technologies for the same reason.

Having a multibillion-dollar company on your cap table can significantly elevate your credibility. They can help with market entry and be cornerstone clients too. Yet CVCs can be slow-moving, and their strategic direction from the top can change, leaving you in a difficult position. They may also put restrictions on what you can do and who you can work with that cut interesting potential opportunities. Each CVC will have ways of working, so make sure you talk to portfolio company founders to get insight into their experience. If your goal is to be acquired, a CVC could be a good place to build a relationship which someday becomes an acquisition.

Summary

- Grants allow you to gain free money when you meet specific criteria.

- R&D Tax Credits allow you to claim back some of your tax if you are eligible.

- Pitch competitions can help you gain small amounts of funding while practising your pitching.

- Non-equity crowdfunding lets you get supporters to fund you while you offer rewards in return.

- Startup-specific loans can have higher interest rates than general loans, but may come with significant support too.

- Revenue-based financing gives you more flexibility in repaying loans.

- Venture debt is for later-stage startups to extend their runway.

- Friends and family are the first investors in your company - be sure to let them know the risks.

- Equity crowdfunding allows the general public to invest in your company, though fees can be expensive.

- Angel investors are individuals who invest in early-stage companies for a wide range of reasons.

- Angel syndicates are groups of angel investors who work together and can provide significant network benefits.

- Startup accelerators and incubators are structured programmes which can give investment as well as support.

- Family offices are institutions created by wealthy families to invest their wealth in a regulated and structured way - they write bigger checks than most angels.

- Venture capital is offered by firms that raise money from other investors and invest on their behalf and bet on potential 100x returns.

- Corporate Venture Capitalists are the venture arms of large companies that look to either diversify or leverage the ecosystem for innovation.

Exercises

- Start listening to founders talk about how they funded their businesses and what they learned.

- When networking, see if you can learn about their experiences with anything they wouldn't say publicly.

- Start mapping out potential investors and understanding their theses.

Chapter 11
Pitching investors

The best way to get funded is to have a startup worth funding. This is what I've been preparing you for since the introduction. You've got the core of your pitch already if you look at Chapter 7's One Page Startup script. Timing is key. You want to raise while you're winning, so you get desirable terms. Investors can take advantage if they smell desperation on you.

Get the concept of investors being "good" or "bad" out of your head. Their job is to make money from their portfolio. Your job is to make money from your customers. They'd obviously rather invest with conditions which legally stack in their favour. If you want more negotiation power, then be more compelling so investors have to fight over you.

The top VCs see thousands of deals a year, and choose only the top few to back. It's not a uniform distribution. The smoking hot startups are chased by VCs, while the hot, lukewarm and freezing cold startups chase the VCs. The blunt truth is that most pitches are so weak they're forgotten in seconds. Let's give you a fighting chance. You need to not only be a startup worth investing in, but a startup which can communicate this to investors.

4 C's Checklist

Use this checklist every time you interact with investors to guide you to giving them what they care about. You want them to think your startup is:

- **Clear** - People should know exactly what you're building and what every slide means. You've lost them the moment they get confused.

- **Credible** - Prove you're the kind of person who can build a successful company in this specific area.

- **Contagious** - Your idea should feel exciting, like something that will spread. Investors should catch your enthusiasm and want to tell their team about you!

- **Commercial** - You're not pitching for charity donations. Your startup should have a clear path to making the investor a return!

When you practice pitching, ask people to explain how they rank your pitch in each category and why. You're in trouble if they can't tell you how they think you're going to make money minutes after listening to you. Or you need better friends. Hopefully the former.

The Traction-Team Tilt

The unwritten rule of what's important to investors at different stages:

- Pre-Series A = Team

- Series A+ = Traction

I want to reframe this for you. When investors assess your team, they're looking at your personal traction *before* whatever startup you're pitching. Are you the person who's going to build a company which will make me rich? Your solution will probably need to change. Do I believe you can pivot and weather the storm or not? They use your past for best guesses when your startup is too early to have anything for them to analyse in-depth.

At Series A+, you should have a mountain of data about your startup's performance. They don't need to guess based on your previous achievements anymore. Yet, in tough funding conditions, you need traction at the earlier stages too if your team isn't convincing enough. People won't tell you to avoid an argument. The weaker your cofounding team's track record, the stronger the traction you'll need for investors. I call this the Traction-Team Tilt. The likes of exited founders, early unicorn employees and mainstream celebrities don't need any traction to raise silly money. As an outsider, you might need more traction than others. You can cry about the world being unfair or start proving your talent.

How the process works

Contrary to what people seem to think in my inbox, you don't get funding by spamming people with coffee requests or asking for quick calls (that are never quick). You need substance to prove you're serious.

Before pitching:

1. Build a data room (pitch deck, cap table, financial data, legal docs).

2. Create a short forwardable summary of the key information.

3. Get feedback from friendly investors/mentors.

4. Record yourself pitching and self-analyse.

5. Iterate your deck and include answers to hard questions.

6. Make target lists for relevant investors.

7. Leverage open submission forms and warm connections.

8. Cold outreach to target investors.

The summary

You're wasting your time asking investors for coffees or calls without any context. You're wasting your time asking your network for warm introductions, too. Anyone who's in demand has to value their time more highly to function. You're obsessed with your startup, but I meet thousands of people like that a year. You've got to stand out.

You've got less than 30 seconds to convince an investor to look at your pitch deck. If your pitch deck is the trailer for your startup, the summary is the trailer for the trailer. Leverage the one-page plan here in its most concise form possible. Every single word should have a purpose and help you get a reply; if it doesn't, cut it. There are many reasons why you might be ignored, and not all have to do with you:

- They didn't understand what you're pitching.
- They've seen the idea before.
- They're not actively investing.
- They don't invest in your type of startup.
- They don't see potential in your market.
- They've backed your direct competitor.
- They don't think you have an edge.

You're not entitled to a reply from anyone. You can track to see if your message was opened. If it was and they ignored you, then there's rarely any point in following up. Their lack of response was a response. Try again when you've got more traction or you've repositioned.

After pitching

The path diverges depending on how interested they are. A powerful investor might just write the check there and then, but don't hold your breath. If they are interested, there's usually due diligence and further checks to be done before terms are offered. The earliest investors can be informal, but insist on legal tracking for your peace of mind. You have two types of funding offers:

- **Unpriced** - Through the use of convertibles, the investors "invest" without knowing how much of the company they'll own. The industry standard is SAFEs in the US and ASAs in the UK. As soon as you close a priced equity round, the instrument converts, and investors are given clarity. Most angel investors invest in this way.

- **Priced** - A set valuation is agreed so the investor knows exactly how much they own of your startup. Your first priced equity round will be from a lead investor who offers a "term sheet", which covers a lot of complex legal stuff. These generally take more time, and you should have competent lawyers on your side.

Unpriced equity is beautiful for founders because it lands in your account much faster and is much less complex. Some investors won't commit until you have a lead investor, because it gives them greater security. It can be frustrating for you, but you should be able to understand why they want this from their perspective.

Valuations

Founders can squabble over valuations in the early days for too long. The truth is, your startup is worth as much as investors are willing to pay. You can do financial gymnastics to justify any price. There's the VC method, the Berkus method, comparable analysis, the first Chicago method and others. It's too high if no one bites.

You don't want to give up more of your startup than you need to by valuing too low. Outsiders think the highest valuation is the greatest win, but you could be setting yourself up for failure. You can become a zombie if you need to raise again and you haven't gained the traction to earn a higher valuation. Existing investors won't reinvest, and new ones will see you overpriced last time. Ouch.

When it comes to negotiating your first priced round, take advice from experts who know your space well and who are qualified to advise you. The best way to not get screwed over is to have several term sheet offers, then you can compare.

Pitch deck slides

Here I'll run through the slides in the general order they're seen in the average pitch deck. Yet it's wise to adapt the order of slides to reflect your strongest case. You have a winner for your first slide if you already have £10m in revenue bootstrapped in two months. Nobody cares about the rest if you can show something that incredible upfront.

1. Welcome slide

Simple, clean. Your name, your startup's name, and a one-liner that explains everything in a quick way. From that one-liner, investors should know your industry, your problem, and roughly what you do.

2. Problem [Chapter 2]

You need to explain as unambiguously as possible while being as concise as you can. Take the time to iterate this slide over and over again to make the message powerful. If people in the room haven't experienced the problem themselves, show them why it's urgent. You're solving a hair-on-fire problem, right? Prove it. Make investors want to solve it now. To help you use either:

- **A shocking story** - Make them feel the pain the customer does. Ideally, it's your story or someone close to you.

- **A shocking statistic** - The investor should want to check the number because it seems unbelievable, and be amazed when it's real. Original research can make you stand out here.

3. Solution [Chapter 3]

Show how you're solving the problem. It must be directly connected to the problem you just described. It should be obvious why your solution works, and it should be 10x better than existing alternatives.

4. Product [Chapter 3]

Show why your solution is unique and game-changing. Use demos, screenshots, or user stories to make it tangible. Mention patents or defensible technology if you have them as well.

5. Market size [Chapter 2]

This slide is often done poorly. Its purpose is to show that your market is big enough for investors to make meaningful returns. The standard is:

- **TAM (Total Addressable Market)** – the entire category.

- **SAM (Serviceable Addressable Market)** – the segment you're targeting.

- **SOM (Serviceable Obtainable Market)** – what you can realistically capture in the next few years.

Avoid lazy "top-down" numbers from reports. Use a "bottom-up" approach: start with your pricing and customer base, then scale up. That's more credible. For example:

- Your annual revenue per customer is £100. You multiply this by the customer segment to estimate the sizes.

- Your target customer is women over 55, ~1 billion people, so your TAM is £100bn.

- You're focusing on the UK, where there are 11 million people in this demographic, so your SAM is £1.1bn.

- You think you can capture 1% of the SAM in the medium term, so your SOM is £11m.

- These numbers aren't accurate, but they show investors there's both long-term and short-term potential.

To push the case for "why now?" then include evidence if the problem has recently become more intense or widespread. E.g., Climate change means there's more hot weather, so demand for household cooling solutions will boom.

6. Team [Chapter 1]

Investors are backing you. Focus on yourself and your cofounders first. Don't just put company logos like Google and Deloitte. Millions of people have worked there. Instead, explain what you achieved there. For example: "Led a project at Google worth $1bn." That proves credibility.

Highlight exceptional achievements outside of business. Are you an Olympian? Cancer-survivor? World record holder? The rarer the achievement, the more interesting it is for an investor. You become more memorable for your talent as opposed to the clones who just assert without evidence that they're resilient.

It's worth including if you've hired top talent who left high-paying jobs to join you, as it signals you can attract A-players. Advisors and board members only matter if they are truly exceptional and relevant. A fintech startup with the CEO of a household name bank on the board will stand out.

7. Traction [Chapter 7]

There's a lot of fake traction in decks, which causes investors to zone out. The best forms of traction in order:

- Revenue (especially recurring revenue with low churn).

- High-value users or customers.

- Testimonials from respected names in your market.

- Waitlists or pre-orders (better if people have already paid).

Awards and pitch competitions don't count as much as people think. Paying customers win every day.

8. Go-to-Market / Distribution [Chapter 4]

How will you actually reach customers? Which sales channels will you use? What's your CAC (customer acquisition cost)? Highlight if you have a unique distribution edge. Social media presence only matters if followers convert into customers.

9. Competition [Chapter 4]

This isn't about proving you're "better." It's about showing you're different. Investors want to see:

- Who the players are.
- How you're positioned.
- Your edge.

Having competitors is good because it proves demand exists. The key is showing why you'll win where they can't.

10. Business model [Chapter 6]

How exactly do you make money? Why did you choose that model? Be ready to justify your answers here. You can include revenue forecasts here, but they're useless unless you've got an engine going. Most decks seem to show everyone as miraculously making £5m revenue after three years. Investors know it will be wrong, but they will be interested in how you got to the numbers.

11. The ask

Don't leave investors guessing what you want from them. This slide should show:

1. **How much you're raising** - Founders give up 10-15% equity per full round, so investors will reverse engineer your valuation range if you don't have a lead investor yet.

2. **How much is already committed** - You might think of investors as lions, but a chunk act like sheep. If you've already got the majority of the round committed, they'll be influenced to jump on too.

3. **What you'll use it for** - Be prepared to justify why you need the money, especially in the age of AI. Could AI reduce your hiring costs? Are you maximising revenue per employee? How will it help you to achieve your target milestones? What are your next steps?

Founder-investor fit

Acquisitions and IPOs can take a long time. You might have a relationship with your first backers longer than the average marriage! You want the right people around you, and you can put investors into three buckets:

- **Saboteur** - Gets in the way and creates pain for the founders.

- **Silent** - Gets out of the way, and you don't hear from them.

- **Supporter** - Gets behind the founders and helps where they can.

Founder expectations of investor contributions are becoming unrealistic. The rise of the AI-generated feel-good thought leadership content from investors doesn't help. You can only be selective about who's on your cap table when your startup is hot enough to have the choice in the first place. You may regret turning down silent investors. Don't be too optimistic about supportive investors. When I started investing in startups, I had the best intentions to get involved, but now I'm too busy with my own company to do as much as I hoped. The founder should always know the problem and customers better than the investor does.

Do your due diligence on anyone you pitch to. Talk to their portfolio companies, especially the ones that failed. How did the investor react under pressure? Avoid saboteur investors unless you'd have to go bust otherwise. If you want strategic help from supporters, then be clear and concise in your ask. Use the principles from Chapter 8.

Summary

- Focus on building a world-class startup, and people will want to invest.

- Whenever interacting with investors, ensure your startup is clear, credible, contagious and commercial in their eyes.

- The weaker your cofounding team's track record, the stronger the traction you'll need for investors.

- Before cold-pitching, set up all your documents correctly and iterate your deck based on feedback from friendly players and your own analysis.

- The 30-second written summary portraying the key information about your startup is underrated - nail this.

- Unpriced equity offers are convertibles where an investor hands over money without knowing exactly what they'll get in return.

- Priced equity rounds will be from your first lead institutional investor and will set a valuation - these tend to take longer and cost more in lawyer fees.

- Overvaluing your startup early is a problem if you don't grow into it and can't raise another round.

- Undervaluing your startup means you give away more of your company than you should have!

- Nail your pitch deck focusing on the 4 C's and Traction-Team Tilt.

- Investor-founder relationships can last a long time; make sure you trust them!

Exercises

- Get used to assessing pitch decks against the criteria I've laid out - there are thousands of examples online.

- Practice adapting your One-Page Startup script into your 30-second summary.

- Start following and interacting with potential investors using the methods from Chapter 8.

Chapter 12
Winning when you exit

Everyone talks about how to start a company, but you'd be smart to think about how to exit one too. Your role changes significantly as the startup grows, and you may prefer the scrappy early days to the later stages. Maybe your personal circumstances have changed, and running your startup is no longer the path which feels right for you. It doesn't mean you've given up on your vision; it just means you're not the best person for it anymore. A happy exit should mean everyone wins:

- Financial freedom for you.

- Return on capital for investors.

- Rewards for sacrifices for employees.

- Greater resources for your customers.

A bad exit can leave you with a sour taste and nights wondering about what-if. Your exit strategy will adapt over time, and investors expect this. Yet having some idea of the destination helps you to make wise decisions today to keep the options open. Employees with equity will appreciate you thinking ahead too!

Types of exits

Let's first look at the different types of exits available. There are more edge cases, but these are the most common:

- Shutting down
- Secondaries
- Acquisitions
  - Acquihire
  - Financial Buy
  - Strategic Buy
- IPO

Shutting down

The brutal truth is your first startup will most likely exit by shutting down. You may struggle for some time before concluding that it's not worth continuing. Take a long view, and avoid the mistake of holding on too long to avoid perceived shame.

You can apply the lessons learned and start again fresh if you choose to. You'll have grown during the journey and be a stronger future founder. I know incredible founders who had a series of failures before striking big. No one remembers what they did 10 years ago. Try to end everything the best you can. Wrap up legal loose ends and communicate with stakeholders to avoid damaging relationships. Be cautious about plastering "exited founder" on your next startup's pitch deck. You don't want people to assume it's a big financial win and feel misled. You'll gain more respect for having the guts to be transparent!

Secondaries

During Chapter 11, I explained that you create new shares for investors rather than selling existing shares. There is nuance. You can sell part of or your entire stake before the company goes public through secondaries. You can have a full or partial exit. Whether this is an option depends on your investors, as they can block it depending on the terms you signed. From their perspective:

- **Pro:** Founders gain greater personal liquidity. They no longer need to worry about their finances and can focus on growing the company. A VC-backed founder has shares worth millions but might still be paying themselves a low salary. This can make large transactions like mortgages tough.

- **Con:** Founders have less financial commitment to the company's future. If they are financially free, they could decide to work less hard, which devalues the startup.

I'm biased in favour of the founders. I don't want you to stress out about money at home when you're running a startup. A word of caution. Some founders have made life-changing money through secondaries, then initiated mass firings. There's a balance here, and you need to be aware of your options.

Secondaries can be a way for early-stage investors to cash out and make space on the cap table for later-stage investors. They can help with employee liquidity in much the same way as founders.

Acquisitions

Though everyone seems to say they're targeting an IPO, acquisitions are much more common and realistic for most founders. There's more than meets the eye, and not all deals are equal.

You might imagine you sign the deal and you're instantly rich, but pure cash deals can be difficult. Often, it's less of an immediate gain with stock in the acquiring company forming part of the deal. The better your company's performance, the better your negotiating position. While all cash might sound great, if your acquirer is a rocket ship itself, then you might be better off long-term with their stock. Let's say Amazon bought you in 2005. Both can be tied to specific performance metrics to ensure safety for the acquirer. There can be retention bonuses to encourage founders and team members to stick around. Here are the main buckets of acquisitions:

Acquihire

When you see someone has sold for an undisclosed amount, then it's likely an acquihire. The product may not have been gaining traction, the bank account may have been getting bare, or the founder's patience may have been wearing thin. The acquirer wants to bring the founders and/or team across and isn't bothered about the product. This can feel damning. Yet market changes can knock out even well-positioned startups with a fantastic team. I told you early on how important luck is. These usually aren't big financial wins, but can give the founders and team a new home. Founders scream from the rooftops about how much they made if they want people to know.

Financial buy

Your brand and mission matter to you as a founder, but it doesn't matter to all potential acquirers, such as private equity firms. Financial buyers will see your company as just a series of numbers. They'll do the maths to work out if they can make a consistent profit or flip you for a higher sum in the future. It's a cold-blooded approach. You might disagree with it, but you didn't think capitalism was sunshine and rainbows, did you? You have the power to turn down these offers and wait for a strategic buy, but there's always risk.

Strategic buy

You're probably hoping for an acquisition in this category. These are usually after product-market fit, whereas the others can be before. Your acquirer buys you because they love your startup and want to integrate it into their offering. Reasons for a strategic buy:

- **Tech** - Your product, when integrated with theirs, gives them a competitive edge.

- **Market access** - You shine in an area where they need help, whether it's geographic or another type of segment. It could also be a horizontal or vertical move.

- **Customers** - Your customer base is their ICP, and they want to sell more to them.

- **Brand** - People love you, and they have a strong product which would sell better when associated with you.

- **Efficiency** - Where there are marginal cost savings from scale, it can make sense for an acquisition to improve profit margins.

- **Competitive** - Your niche is close to theirs, and you're swapping each other's companies. By acquiring you, they may be able to increase customer loyalty and their prices.

Most buys are in the millions and tens of millions. The goliath deals worth millions make headline news. The more valuable you are, the fewer potential buyers you have. Big tech companies now have cash reserves to vacuum up almost anyone. For you to win, they need to see value in buying you rather than outcompeting you. Speed is the core advantage of buying rather than building.

IPOs

Initial Public Offerings (IPOs) are seen as the dream. You list on a major stock exchange like the London Stock Exchange or NASDAQ for a valuation in the billions. Yet such IPOs are rare. The market goes through bumper seasons and quiet ones. Sometimes, it's a matter of timing.

Public companies are held to different standards than private companies. This is because only qualified people can invest in private companies, whereas anyone can buy public shares, which means the governments want more safeguards in place. Transparency about revenues and costs can also be alarming to some founders. To go public, you start by hiring underwriters from investment banks, who will then walk you through the process. General advice is to shop around and only work with a bank you trust.

IPOs can come much earlier in a startup's life than founders realise. You can use listings like a growth round where the public is investing rather than venture capitalists. You'll need friendly investors to do so, but it can provide a stress-busting injection of liquidity when done right. Public investors get quarterly updates but don't exert the power or control you can get from VCs. The rules vary depending on your area, and it's worth being up to date on them once you hit scale.

Exit planning

You now know the best way to get funding is by being a startup worth funding. Exits are much the same. The best way to earn a happy exit is by being a startup which is worth a happy exit. The majority of the work is running your company well, but here are further tips:

Be aligned

Exits can turn messy if key players want different outcomes. Have regular alignment conversations. Your cofounders, investors, and employees must be on the same page. Through your cap table, you know who owns what. Ensure you're aware of the preferential treatment some investors have. VCs can protect their downside risk and block exits if you sign terms which let them. VCs work on the power law. They're incentivised to push for a mega return rather than take an early "okay" exit.

Be clean

No one wants to buy and integrate a chaotic company, and you can't IPO if your books are a mess. If you've already been running your company for a while, you'll know the pain of tax and legal issues. It's vital these are dealt with before looking at exits.

This means having clear financial records and no dodgy missing money or financial "tricks." Use proper accountancy software and taxes, payroll and VAT systematised. Use standard employment contracts without any abnormal clauses. Have defensible IP. Protect your brand. Update everything at least quarterly. Get an external body to ensure you're compliant.

Be obsolete

"You either die a hero or live long enough to become the villain."
Harvey Dent, The Dark Knight

You want to exit before everyone else needs you to leave! If you make the company too dependent on you, then your exit options become limited. You'll need to put blood, sweat and tears into building the company, but you should become obsolete at a mature stage. Any competent CEO should be able to continue your work and your mission. Build a leadership team capable of running the company without you.

Make the company as systems-oriented as you can after you get through the messy phase. The clearer processes and systems you have in place, the easier the business is to take over. If you want to be acquired, you need to be acquirable.

Be alert

Track who could buy you and have a good relationship with them once you hit product-market fit. They might be your competition, but one day they could be the ones who make you rich. Make sure people know who you are and that your company is doing well. Become friends with people in:

- Corporate development teams
- Family offices
- PE funds
- Executives of companies in your niche

You want to keep updating the list of acquirers regularly as the industry shifts. What is the acquisition history in your sector? What size companies tend to be bought? Who are the major players? Why are they acquiring?

Be open

By the time a serious exit opportunity comes along, you'll have worked hard on your startup, and it might be hard to let go. You might reject life-changing sums out of pride or ego. Timing is everything. You'll think you can keep growing the company and getting a better exit until one day you can't. You then might end up selling for less than you could have accepted in the past. You want to be bought, not sold.

Summary

- Come to terms with the fact that you might not lead your startup forever.

- You can shut down, take secondaries, get acquired, or go public through an IPO.

- Shutting down is a stepping stone to future success; don't let shame overcome you.

- Secondaries are where you can sell some or all of your shares while the company remains private to other investors.

- Acquihires are generally where a company can't reach product-market fit or loses fit and is acquired for the team.

- Financial buys are where the acquirer doesn't care about the mission but sees it as a profitable asset.

- Strategic buys are where the acquirer wants the product and brand you've built, and are usually the best financial outcomes for acquisitions.

- IPOs are where you list on a stock exchange and can be the most significant outcome for founders, yet you can explore listing earlier, depending on your market.

- Ensure all owners of the company are aligned on the exit direction.

- Keep your books clean and your name away from the courts.

- As you scale, hire a leadership team which can make you obsolete.
- Don't let ego get in the way of a good exit.

Exercises

- Research exits in the spaces you're looking to enter.

- Map out who potential acquirers could be someday and what would make you attractive to them.

- Ground your expectations of what an exit could look like and plan your finances accordingly.

- Don't forget to dare to dream!

Conclusion and Thanks

You've made it to the end! That's it. You're now primed to take action.

Your ability to execute is the most significant factor in whether your startup will succeed. Get your head into the game. Take care to assess cofounders to improve execution. Look at their mindset, their values, their long-term vision and their competencies.

Obsess over problems and customers, not solutions. To build something people need, you have to understand them first.

Iterate from simple non-functional MVPs, all the way to a full-featured product. Don't be afraid to launch early and prioritise quick feedback loops over all else.

Earn attention from potential customers by experimenting with different channels and doubling down on what works. Remember, you don't need to have a personal brand.

Keep your costs under control and know your numbers. Decide on a business model or models which can scale. Don't be afraid to make messy money in the meantime to stay alive.

Use short-term and long-term goals to prevent being overwhelmed by all the noise. Be aware of signals you need to pivot, and act decisively if you pull the trigger.

Leverage my One Page Startup script to gain clarity. Repeat it as many times as you need to, as your assumptions are proven incorrect.

Who you know matters, but network like a pro using the RSVP formula. Be resourceful to ask good questions. Be specific so people can assess you fairly. Be visible to build familiarity. Be powerful to attract inbound.

When it's time to hire, choose well; they determine the culture for everyone who comes after them. Delay hiring as long as you can. PMF is a good signal.

Take external funding to accelerate your scaling if you can use it well. But leverage the cheapest forms first, rather than jumping straight to venture capital.

When pitching, it's best to have a startup worth investing in rather than looking for hacks. The Traction-Team Tilt is the key lesson. If you don't have an all-star background, then you will need more traction.

Think about how you want the journey to end. You aren't selfish for wanting a good financial outcome, and you want someone who will hopefully continue your mission.

Acknowledgments

First and foremost, thank you to my family for all the love and support throughout my life. The lessons my pops taught me while he was alive will stay with me forever. I dedicate this book to him and hope it helps many of you. I think he'd like that. Extra special shout-out to my mum, who is the strongest person I know.

Massive appreciation to my cofounder, Gurvir Riyat. Bae HQ wouldn't be possible without him. Whenever I've used "I" throughout this book, it's really been "we", but it's odd for me to talk as a collective. His fingerprints and knowledge are all over these pages - trust me!

Thank you to all the beta readers and those who gave me feedback on the drafts of this book. This includes Stephen Moore, Neda Sahebelm, Anisha Parmar, Malika Arshad, Uzma Rafiq, Anisah Osman Britton MBE, Aishwarya Agarwalla, Grishma Patel, Mehwish Shoukat, Amber Nasir, Nitika Vyas, Kavita Varma, Bhagirathi Shah, Rajiv Samani, Anand Dattani, Annabel Pemberton, Dr. Veena Babu, Natalie Yuan and Nikita Parekh.

Many people have believed in me and guided me at various stages of my journey. I couldn't possibly name them all here, but I appreciate you all. This includes everyone who's been on the podcasts or spoken at our events.

Thank you to everyone who's come before me and shared their knowledge to help outsiders break into startups. My knowledge comes from internalising mountains of content from others. I hope I've given everyone credit when sharing their frameworks! Thank you to Rob Fitzpatrick, who wrote "Write Useful Books" and made this whole process much simpler for me.

Thank you

Last but not least, thank you. I'm a random outsider who was never interested in startups, yet I ended up writing a book about them. I'm humbled you chose to pick up this book, and it gave you enough value to make it to the end. I'd love for you to leave a review or recommendation. If you send a selfie and a 100-word review to amar@thebaehq.com, there's a chance I'll add you to startupsforoutsiders.com. I wish you the absolute best in your startup journey, and I hope you make a positive difference in the world. Have a great day.

Amardeep Parmar

Printed in Dunstable, United Kingdom